The United States
and the
Italo-Ethiopian Crisis

The United States
and the
Italo-Ethiopian Crisis

BRICE HARRIS, JR.

Stanford University Press
Stanford, California
1964

Preface

The Italo-Ethiopian crisis of 1934–36 initiated a chain of events in Europe that culminated in the Second World War. Fascist Italy succeeded in conquering and annexing the last independent African state in defiance of the League of Nations, Great Britain, and world public opinion. As a result of the eighteen-month crisis, a realignment of European powers developed. The League of Nations collapsed, helpless in the face of wanton aggression and unrestricted rearmament. The efforts of the United States at cooperation were limited by Congress at home and ignored by powers abroad, and the American people were further convinced of European intrigue and perfidy.

Shortly after the Italian invasion of Ethiopia on October 3, 1935, Elmer Davis predicted in a letter to the *New York Times* "that whatever happens it will all be Uncle Sam's fault. If Mussolini is stopped by sanctions or the British fleet, every Italian will remember that this could never have happened if America had supported its traditional policy" of freedom of the seas. If Mussolini is not stopped, and if the British "decide to make the best of the situation by dividing Haile Selassie's assets with the aggressor, every Englishman will know that the need of assuming this repugnant added burden of empire is due solely to America's failure to support Britain's altruistic policy."

What part did the United States, the world's greatest power though not a member of the League of Nations, play in the Italo-Ethiopian debacle? Was the lack of positive and forthright American cooperation responsible for the failure of the League of Nations to restrain Mussolini, or did the reasons lie rather in the relations among the nations of Europe, the personalities of their leaders, and the hopes and fears of their people? What did the United States do in the Italo-Ethiopian crisis? Could it have done more? The following chapters will seek to untangle the international threads of the crisis with emphasis on the policy, action, and responsibility of the United States.

I wish to express my deepest appreciation to Professors Ernest R. May and Frank Freidel of Harvard University, under whose able guidance this study began; to my father, Brice Harris, Professor of English at Arizona State University, who reviewed the entire manuscript; to Cornelius Van H. Engert, American Minister to Ethiopia in 1936, who read the text and gave me his personal comments; to the San Diego State College Foundation for a grant-in-aid which permitted me to accomplish additional research and revision; to my typists, Dorothy Ramsey and Frances Gandolfo, and of course my wife, Carolyn, who did more than type; and to scores of other persons and libraries for assisting me in many ways. I am indebted to all of them—and to Ethiopia.

B. H.

Contents

If men were all virtuous, returned the artist, I
should with great alacrity teach them all to fly. But
what would be the security of the good, if the bad could
at pleasure invade them from the sky? Against an army
sailing through the clouds neither walls, nor mountains,
nor seas, could afford any security. A flight of northern
savages might hover in the wind, and light at once with
irresistible violence upon the capital of a fruitful
region that was rolling under them. Even this valley,
the retreat of princes, the abode of happiness, might be
violated by the sudden descent of some of the naked nations
that swarm on the coast of the southern sea.

—SAMUEL JOHNSON, *Rasselas,*
Prince of Abissinia (1759)

Chapter One

The Background of the Crisis and the Incident at Wal-Wal

A restless soldier's random shot at a bird, one of the arbitrators later suggested, may have triggered the border incident at Wal-Wal, marking the beginning of the Italo-Ethiopian crisis of 1934–36.[1] On December 5, 1934, some 600 colonial troops from Italian Somaliland and 1,500 Ethiopians clashed for control of the strategic wells of Wal-Wal in Ethiopia's arid southeastern triangle. All maps, including those recently issued by the Italian Ministry of Colonies, clearly located Wal-Wal some 60 miles within Ethiopian territory, but the actual boundary had never been determined formally. Pastoral tribes from both sides of the undemarcated frontier used the important wells. Without protest from the Ethiopian government, which had never exercised effective authority in this steppe region, Italian forces had gradually encroached upon the area from Somaliland and had established a military post at Wal-Wal in 1928.[2]

The Italian troops occupying Wal-Wal in late 1934 were Somali askaris commanded by an Italian officer. The Ethiopian force had escorted the Anglo-Ethiopian Boundary Commission, which had just completed actual demarcation of the border between Ethiopia and British Somaliland and was now investigating nomadic and grazing problems. The Italian commander at Wal-Wal refused to permit the Commission to use the wells, which the Ethiopians adamantly protested were in Ethiopian territory. The British contingent thereupon withdrew in order not to become involved in the dispute. Italian and Ethiopian troops exchanged insults for almost two weeks until the inevitable clash on December 5. Several Italian tanks and airplanes forced the more numerous Ethiopians to retreat with heavy losses.

Such incidents often arise along undefined borders in arid, underpopulated regions where water is vital and authority loose. In itself the Wal-Wal incident seemed unimportant and susceptible of settlement by patience and good will. Fascist Italy, however, which for some time had been planning to expand its colonial holdings, seized this fortuitous opportunity to proclaim to the world Ethiopian irresponsibility and aggression. Self-defense demanded that Italy reinforce its two East African colonies bordering on Ethiopia: Eritrea to the north and Italian Somaliland to the southeast.

Italian Fascism had entered a new and important phase in the early 1930's, one shaped by its ideology and the personality of its leader, Benito Mussolini. The first decade of Fascist rule in Italy was spent consolidating the party's power at home. Italian foreign policy, however, had shown signs of independence. Italy was the first European power to recognize the Soviet Union, and managed to rally Austria and Hungary into a circle of client states by supporting revision of the World War treaties. In retrospect, Italy's truculent seizure of Corfu and short-lived defiance of the League of Nations in 1923 hinted ominously at later events. Nevertheless, during the 1920's domestic problems were paramount. Mussolini appeared content to leave foreign affairs to such men as the career diplomat Salvatore Contarini, Secretary General of the Italian Foreign Office until 1925, and the moderate Fascist Dino Grandi, Foreign Minister from 1929 to 1932, both of whom favored cooperation with Great Britain and the League of Nations.[3]

By the 1930's the party and its leader had established themselves as the masters of Italy. Fascism, which in 1928 Mussolini had emphasized was not for export, became by 1932 the ideal governmental system, a system that would spread inevitably throughout Europe. In a series of speeches he warned that Italy would not remain forever a prisoner of the Mediterranean, that Italy saw its destiny to the south and east as a unifying bridge between Europe and Africa and Asia, and that a fully armed Italy would soon force other nations to choose between its precious friendship and its fierce hostility.[4]

This new emphasis on colonialism and national greatness can be explained in part by Mussolini's inability to resolve domestic problems, by the worldwide economic depression, and by Italy's overpopulation in relation to its natural resources. But Mussolini's Fascism assumed a far more important role. Fascist ideology required the construction of a new, universal, and perfect empire, a third Rome, which would solve men's problems and create material prosperity for all. Fascism's duty and destiny, its adherents proclaimed, were to recapture the glory of ancient Rome and to restore the imperial city to its former greatness. This nostalgia for ancient Rome, always a prime factor in Italian thinking, became an obsession in the 1930's.[5]

Closely associated with Fascist ideology was the yearning for greatness, both personal and national. The son of a Romagna blacksmith, Mussolini spoke for millions less articulate than himself when he assailed the more fortunate, whether other Italians or foreign nations. "It is impossible to trace any coherent principle behind [Mussolini's] actions, beyond the fanatical and almost pathetic desire to make his country and himself great during his own lifetime."[6]

Most assessments of Mussolini characterize him as bold in language and appearance, opportunistic in policy, but cautious in action. Favorite examples of his timidity are his anxiety before the March on Rome in 1922 and his hesitancy after the murder of political foe Matteotti in 1924. In both cases more militant Fascists forced or strengthened his hand.[7] Yet in the Italo-Ethiopian crisis Mussolini was anything but timid. Instead, he appeared as a determined dictator, rejecting concessions and insisting throughout on the whole prize despite the advice of his own Foreign Office and the pleas of his erstwhile allies.

After the final pacification of Libya in 1931, Italy took a renewed interest in its two older East African colonies. Early in 1932 General Emilio de Bono, an early Fascist and now Minister of the Colonies, traveled to Eritrea at Mussolini's request to study conditions in Italy's first colony. Everything depended, reported de Bono, upon the ultimate goal of Fascism in East Africa. "In 1932 nothing definite had as yet been settled as regards the character and method of a possible campaign against the probable enemy." Italy would have to decide "whether it was our intention to initiate operations by assuming a posture of defence, or whether we should take the offensive without more ado." De Bono's memoirs clearly indicate that as early as 1932 Fascism sought colonial expansion at Ethiopia's expense, and that both he and Mussolini had agreed on this.[8]

Later in 1932, Mussolini himself replaced Dino Grandi as Foreign Minister because, as he later explained, "Geneva had an extremely bad influence on him and he came to espouse the cause of the League of Nations."[9] Grandi's pro-English moderation was out of step with the evolving Fascist foreign policy, which stressed Italian prestige and expansion. Even after Grandi's demotion, however (he was named ambassador to Great Britain), the principal supporting figures in the Foreign Office continued to be non-Fascist or "half-Fascist."[10] The two most important of these career diplomats were Under Secretary Fulvio Suvich and League of Nations Delegate Pompeo Aloisi. Although sympathetic to Mussolini's colonial aspirations, they argued that Italy could and should expand its colonial empire by negotiation with the British and French rather than at the risk of European solidarity.[11]

But the European situation in 1933 seemed to Fascist Italy one from which it could profit only if it moved quickly. Adolf Hitler's rise to power in January and the failure of the Geneva Disarmament Conference in October clearly indicated to Mussolini that he would have to take action before the great powers rearmed.[12] Thus in the fall of 1933 Mussolini definitely determined that he would settle the Ethiopian problem no later than 1936 and have everything ready for the operation by 1935. He assured Austrian Chancellor Kurt von Schuschnigg in mid-1934 that war with Ethiopia was inevitable, that Italy would require only one year for the conquest, and that his troops would return to the Brenner Pass before Hitler could prepare for war. "We still have a few years of breathing space [before Hitler acts], but in 1937, I think, things will begin happening." Early in 1935 Mussolini gave Breckinridge Long, American Ambassador in Rome, "the definite and uneradicable impression that he expects war with Germany within a comparatively short time." Long did not know why Mussolini was preparing for warfare in Ethiopia "unless he thinks it would be good training for his men. Nevertheless, the Abyssinian campaign proceeds and the thought of eventual conflict with Germany continues."[13]

It was not pure chance that Mussolini chose Ethiopia as the area for Italian expansion. Not only was Ethiopia the last remaining independent African state, but Italy had long demonstrated particular interest in the area. In the late-nineteenth-century partition of Africa, Italy had gained a predominant position in the East African horn, a position that included part of the rugged highlands of Ethiopia. But the humiliating defeat inflicted by the Ethiopian Emperor Menelik II on the encroaching Italians at Adowa in 1896 left Italy with bitter memories and only the two small coastal colonies of Eritrea and Somaliland. Since then, Italy had sought with little success to bring the bulk of Ethiopia within the Italian sphere of influence.[14] It seemed obvious for Mussolini to turn to Ethiopia for expansion. What could be better for Fascist prestige than a great victory where Liberal Italy had ignominiously failed? The accidental encounter at Wal-Wal in late 1934 initiated a climactic phase in the long struggle between Italy and Ethiopia.[15]

The Fascists contended that the threat of Ethiopian aggression, as evidenced in the Wal-Wal incident, posed a constant menace to the safety of Eritrea and Somaliland. If the problem were not resolved, it might leave Italy powerless to protect its East African colonies in the event of a European crisis. Peaceful penetration, represented by the Italo-Ethiopian Treaty of Friendship, Conciliation, and Arbitration of 1928, had failed, they alleged, because of Ethiopian obstinacy and bad faith.[16] Fascists and their sympathizers also claimed that overpopulated Italy needed room for its expanding population, especially since the Americas had restricted the normal emigration outlets.[17]

Both arguments had little basis in fact. Throughout the crisis Mussolini had rejected compromises granting Italy widespread economic and settlement concessions. Few Italians had settled in Italy's three existing colonies, although sections of Eritrea were just as suitable for European settlement as Ethiopia. Moreover, though the Fascists had proclaimed the need for more land for Italy's surplus population, they had simultaneously encouraged a greater population increase for purposes of a larger national army. Obviously, the real driving force behind the Ethiopian venture was political. The Wal-Wal episode occurred in the context of

Italy's yearning for recognition as a great power and the memory of the debacle at Adowa.

After Mussolini's fateful decision in the fall of 1933 that operations would begin in late 1935, preparations pushed forward rapidly. Almost everyone in "half-Fascist" circles, from the military chiefs and diplomats to the aristocracy and the royal family, opposed the venture, some secretly, some actively. Mussolini, however, was sure of success.[18] The clash at Wal-Wal, which could not have been more opportune had Italy prearranged it, served as a justification for the greatly increased shipments of manpower and supplies required for the occupation of Ethiopia.

Mussolini expected neither opposition from France, with whom Italy was negotiating a settlement of all outstanding differences, nor any effective objection from Great Britain, the United States, or the League of Nations. The Manchurian crisis had proved to his satisfaction how the world would react to resolute action.[19] The need for Italian cooperation in Europe, Mussolini considered, would persuade Great Britain, France, and the Soviet Union to acquiesce in Fascist Italy's colonial conquest exactly as they had in Italy's seizure of Tripoli on the eve of the First World War.[20]

After the Wal-Wal clash Italy and Ethiopia charged each other with responsibility for the incident and self-righteously protested the unprovoked attack. As the weaker power, Ethiopia immediately requested arbitration in accordance with the Italo-Ethiopian Treaty of 1928. By its terms the two countries had agreed to submit to arbitration any dispute they could not resolve between themselves. Italy declined, insisting that Ethiopian guilt was clear, and demanded a formal apology and a heavy cash indemnity. The Ethiopian Emperor, Haile Selassie, then asked the Secretary General of the League of Nations to draw the attention of the League Council to the serious situation in East Africa.

On January 3, 1935, the Ethiopian ruler sent a second telegram to Geneva affirming that Italy had massed troops on the borders and killed Ethiopian soldiers, and that Italian planes had menaced Ethiopian villages. Haile Selassie sought now the application of Article 11 of the Covenant of the League of Nations, under which any threat of war became a matter of concern to the entire League. The Secretary General, on the request of any member, had to summon a meeting of the Council. In the meantime, while the Emperor sought arbitration and promised in advance to accept any decision, Mussolini, on December 30, completed a plan for military operations against Ethiopia.[21]

Haile Selassie's request posed delicate problems for the League of Nations and its Anglo-French leadership: how to uphold the rights of the weaker state without offending the stronger, and how to uphold the prestige of the League without losing the cooperation of Italy in Europe. As the most important members of the League, Great Britain and France were chiefly responsible for its policy. Since their colonial territories adjoined Italy's in surrounding Ethiopia, they had long taken an interest in East Africa and had agreed with Italy in the Tripartite Treaty of 1906 to consult on Ethiopian affairs.

But in early 1935, Great Britain and France were far more interested in Hitler's Germany than in Haile Selassie's Ethiopia. No one had forgotten the Italian mobilization on the Brenner Pass only six months previously, when Austrian Chancellor Dollfuss had been murdered and Austrian independence threatened by Nazi Germany. Great Britain and France, still counting on Italy against Hitler, determined to show every consideration to Mussolini. Their ambivalence led to "a sort of dual procedure which in the end proved fatal to the League." For reasons of prestige and propriety they followed a policy of discussion within the world organization, but behind this façade they negotiated directly with Italy in an effort to solve the dispute harmoniously. Britain and France hoped to maintain both the face of the League and the friendship of Italy.[22]

Italy's policy during early 1935 was to lengthen debate by procedural obstacles while its military preparations were being completed. Operations could not commence until the end of the torrential summer rains. Thus, League Delegate Aloisi stubbornly refused arbitration, denying the jurisdiction of the League Council. Mussolini personally instructed Aloisi to yield nothing to Ethiopia and to see that the League did not take up the dispute.[23] Ethiopia, on the contrary, desired to publicize the incident in the hope that an aroused world public opinion, working through the League of Nations, would persuade Italy to seek a peaceful solution.

Anthony Eden, Britain's delegate to the League, and French Foreign Minister Pierre Laval sought to persuade the Ethiopian representative not to place on the Council agenda the Emperor's request for application of Article 11. At the same time they endeavored to draw Mussolini into direct negotiations with Ethiopia. On January 15, in the face of Italian intransigence, the Ethiopian representative finally made the request. To avoid Council discussion Italy had to retreat; on January 19 Aloisi announced Italian readiness to proceed in accordance with the Treaty of 1928. But he had stalled successfully for six weeks. As Mussolini desired, the League had not yet assumed responsibility for the Wal-Wal dispute. Direct negotiations between Italy and Ethiopia could drag out almost indefinitely.

France, in particular, had no desire to challenge or embarrass Italy. In quest of security against a larger and potentially more powerful Germany, France had constructed after 1919 a series of defensive alliances with smaller European states which, like France, had no interest in revising the First World War settlement. Similarly, an increasing fear of Nazi Germany had brought France and Italy together. In early January 1935, Laval journeyed to Rome to negotiate the two countries' outstanding differences.

The Rome Agreements of that month provided for joint Franco-Italian collaboration in support of Austrian independence and for the ultimate surrender of Italian rights in Tunisia. Italy was to receive in exchange a minority of shares in the French-owned Jibuti–Addis Ababa railroad and small territorial additions to Libya and Eritrea. Although the question of Austria was important, Mussolini had an additional reason for a *rapprochement* with France: Ethiopia. The Rome Agreements included a secret written annex by which France renounced all interests in Ethiopia beyond the railroad and its immediate zone.[24]

Did this give Mussolini a free hand in Ethiopia, as he later insisted, or did it mean merely that France would raise no objection to Italian economic penetration or even to a gradual Moroccan-type campaign, as Laval later asserted.[25] The exact content of the private conversation between the two leaders on the night of January 6 at the French Embassy in Rome remains unknown. Sir Robert Vansittart, Permanent Undersecretary of the British Foreign Office, gave his view of the meeting in his memoirs: "A

wink is as good as a nod, and Laval had a drooping lid. . . . De-
vious natures understand each other quickly." In any case, Mussolini felt certain that he had obtained French acquiescence in his
Ethiopian venture, and he acted accordingly.[26]

Most political factions in France welcomed the Rome Agreements as greatly strengthening French security vis-à-vis Germany.
The rise of Hitler had tempered the conciliatory pacifism of the
non-Communist left, which approved the published texts despite
its loathing for Mussolini. The Socialists, however, taking note of
rumors that Laval had granted Mussolini a free hand in Ethiopia,
obtained assurances from the French Foreign Minister that he had
given no such commitment. The Communists continued to oppose
all measures and alliances for French national defense until later
in 1935 when Stalin explicitly blessed French rearmament with
the Franco-Soviet Pact.[27]

The new pact with Italy especially pleased the French right,
partly for ideological reasons but chiefly because of the right's traditional emphasis on a strong alliance system as opposed to reliance
on the League of Nations. To Laval and the right this new Italian
agreement became France's most important alliance for security
in Europe, one to be maintained at any cost.[28]

Thinking he had obtained a free hand from France, Mussolini
turned to Great Britain, Italy's friend and ally since the struggle
for Italian unification. The British had encouraged Italian interest in East Africa in the late nineteenth century as a potential
check on the encroaching French and Sudanese. Except for the
northwestern corner of Ethiopia, which includes the Blue Nile
and Lake Tana, Britain had recognized Italian interests in the
country.

The Rome Agreements between Mussolini and Laval reached
London less than a week after their signature.[29] On January 29
Ambassador Grandi suggested to Undersecretary Vansittart that
Italy would like to exchange ideas with Britain with a view to
assuring "the mutual and harmonious development of Anglo-Italian interests in Abyssinia." The Italians thought Vansittart's response evasive.[30] The British neither accepted the obvious invitation to follow the French example nor told Italy what Britain
would do.

Prompted by Suvich and Aloisi and by his own fear of an Anglo-

Italian break, Grandi sought to engage the British Foreign Office
in similar conversations several times during the late winter and
early spring of 1935. The British consistently responded that while
the government thought Anglo-Italian colonial problems capable
of friendly settlement, British public opinion would oppose any
Italian colonial effort in Ethiopia.[31] But at no time did the British
inform the Italians precisely what action Great Britain would take
if Italy ignored British pleas for compromise.

The British government never misunderstood Mussolini's intentions. "You realize, don't you," Foreign Minister Sir John Simon
remarked cynically to British Ethiopian expert Geoffrey Thompson in January, "that the Italians intend to take Abyssinia."[32]
Immediately after receiving the notice of the Rome Agreements,
Simon had established an interdepartmental committee, chaired
by Sir John Maffey, Permanent Undersecretary for the Colonies,
to investigate British interests in Ethiopia and to consider how an
Italian conquest might affect them. Later, under severe criticism
for the government's equivocal policy, Anthony Eden suggested
weakly that Britain had never responded to the Italian overtures
because the matter was under study by the Maffey Committee.[33]

The Maffey Report, rendered in June 1935, concluded that although an independent Ethiopia would be preferable for Great
Britain, the only national interests involved were the basin of the
Blue Nile and certain grazing rights. Some time after submission
of the secret report, a trusted Italian employee purloined a copy
from the files of the British Embassy in Rome.[34] It would be interesting to know when the document was taken and what encouragement, if any, it gave to Italian stubbornness.

During early 1935 the British government, like the French, concentrated on establishing a new basis for Anglo-German-French
relations.[35] Fear of Germany had led France to come to terms with
Mussolini. Great Britain did not have the same fear of Germany;
indeed, many Englishmen felt that Germany had been treated
harshly at Versailles, and sympathized with Germany's claims to
equality of rights. The British hoped that a regularization of relations might eliminate differences and persuade Hitler to return to
the League of Nations.

Specifically, they hoped that Laval's conciliatory stand on the
Saar plebiscite in late January 1935 might facilitate negotiations

with Germany. In early February, Great Britain and France joined to offer Hitler equality in armaments in return for regional security agreements and an air pact. But Hitler, taking as his pretext the British White Paper of March 4 recommending limited rearmament and a French decree of March 15 extending military service to two years, announced on March 16 the institution of conscription in Germany. This action repudiated Part Five of the Treaty of Versailles and canceled the bargaining point offered by Great Britain and France.

Hitler had not calculated this move to take advantage of divergence among his foes; he had planned it for a year. Germany had taken no interest in the Italo-Ethiopian conflict beyond insisting upon its own strict neutrality.[36] Only later in 1935, when the dispute between Italy and Ethiopia turned into war, did Germany consider how it might use the crisis for its own advantage.

The German announcement of conscription, however, had considerable influence on the Italo-Ethiopian conflict, coming as it did one day before Haile Selassie's St. Patrick's Day appeal to the League. The Ethiopian Emperor asserted that direct negotiations with Italy had failed, that Italy still refused arbitration by the Friendship Treaty of 1928, and that Italy was sending large numbers of soldiers and workers and great quantities of military supplies to Eritrea and Italian Somaliland.[37]

Haile Selassie's unfortunately timed plea[38] was lost in the confusion caused by Hitler's speech. Now, when Italian cooperation against Germany appeared particularly essential, the British and French desired above all not to offend Mussolini. The German action, however, did cause the League to establish a committee to recommend steps to be taken in the event of future treaty-breaking. This committee laid the groundwork for the action taken by the League against Italy later in 1935.

Mussolini, who joined Great Britain and France in protesting Hitler's unilateral repudiation of the Treaty of Versailles, invited their prime ministers and foreign ministers to meet with him and Suvich at Stresa, in the Italian lake country. The moderates in the Italian Foreign Office hoped the occasion might serve to prevent a break over Ethiopia between Italy and Great Britain.[39] Grandi in London persuaded the British Foreign Office to send its Ethiopian expert, Geoffrey Thompson, to Stresa in the hope of fruitful

talks. Nevertheless, the six ministerial delegates did not discuss
the Italo-Ethiopian crisis. The British did not introduce the subject, fearing it would break up the conference. However, lower-
echelon experts, Thompson and his Italian counterpart, G. B.
Guarnaschelli, did broach the matter informally. Guarnaschelli
bluntly volunteered that his country might have to solve the Ethiopian problem by force, to which Thompson cautiously responded
that British public opinion would permit no deal.[40]

The high-level conference at Stresa offered Great Britain its last
opportunity to check Italy at a minimum cost by telling Mussolini
that it strongly disapproved of his intentions in Ethiopia, that it
would oppose aggression, and that it would support the League
of Nations to the hilt. But feeling little pressure yet from public
opinion, Prime Minister MacDonald and Foreign Secretary Simon
believed they saw valid reasons to avoid a divisive issue and thought
it wiser to consider only the immediate problem of Germany.
Later, in the House of Commons Eden rationalized Britain's failure to act, arguing that since Mussolini had agreed in March to
arbitrate the dispute with Ethiopia, no need had arisen to discuss
the subject at Stresa.[41]

When Mussolini read aloud the draft of the final communiqué
of the Stresa Conference, "'after having reviewed all the international questions which are posed . . . ,' he hesitated and asked:
'Should not we add *in Europe*?'" French Premier Pierre Etienne
Flandin thought this a clear invitation to the British to speak of
Ethiopia. "But neither Mr. MacDonald nor Sir John Simon moved
a muscle. M. Laval and I, and without doubt Mussolini as well,
had the impression of a tacit acquiescence given by the British government to the Italian ambitions in Ethiopia."[42]

The careful diplomacy at Geneva, where Great Britain and
France went to great lengths to assuage Mussolini, the silence-
means-consent appearance at Stresa, the fear aroused by Nazi Germany's rearmament program, and the lack of any definite warning
by Britain convinced Mussolini that he would meet little opposition from either the European powers or the League of Nations.
Great Britain might not make the kind of agreement Laval had
made, but Mussolini felt that the facts surely indicated British
assent. Suvich remarked at his trial after the Second World War
that "the Ethiopian War was made by a gentleman's agreement

with England."[43] After the Stresa Conference, Italian preparations
and shipments increased greatly; Mussolini had committed himself
and his country.

Although Italy had agreed in late March to arbitrate the Wal-Wal
incident with Ethiopia, its diplomats had found one reason after
another for not doing so. When the Council of the League met
for its regular monthly session on May 20, the two countries had
not yet selected an arbitration commission. Italy had successfully
stalled for five months. Hugh R. Wilson, the American observer
at Geneva, commented that he had "yet to see the case in which
decisive action was taken unless and until one of the great powers
of Europe carried the banner and campaigned in favor of such
action."[44]

In early 1935 the British government had concentrated on the
problem of Germany, and British public opinion had relaxed in
a holiday mood. The worst of the depression seemed over, and
all looked forward to George V's Jubilee in early May. After the
royal celebration, however, the British public awoke to the Italian
threat and to the government's apparent acquiescence in Mussolini's plans. Mussolini's increasing defiance and the rapid accelera-
tion of Italian troop and supply shipments following the Stresa
Conference angered an aroused British public. It forced the government to take the Italo-Ethiopian dispute seriously.

The British government, controlled since the electoral landslide
of 1931 by a National coalition dominated by Conservatives, had
paid lip service to the League of Nations but had carefully avoided
both political obligations and the enumeration of Britain's responsibilities as a member of the world organization. Most Conservatives—especially the right wing, who were influential in the British
press and the House of Lords—considered the League more a forum
for discussion and compromise than a vehicle for collective action
against violators of the peace. On other issues of foreign policy,
the National government favored limited rearmament, negotiations within or without the League, and an agreement with Germany. The Baldwin cabinet, which took office early in June 1935,
was not a great ministry and like its leader preferred "to wait upon
events rather than to master them."[45]

In Great Britain, as in France, the parties on the left supported

the League of Nations most enthusiastically. The principal opposition party, Labour, had seen its Parliamentary representation
drastically reduced in the depression election of 1931. A pacifist,
doctrinaire minority of the Labour party demanded complete and
unilateral disarmament. The more pragmatic majority wing, led
by Arthur Henderson, Clement Attlee, and trade union leaders,
supported disarmament by international agreement, the establishment of an international police force, and the strengthening of the
collective peace system. A 1934 foreign policy statement by the
National Executive Committee, entitled "Socialism and Peace,"
proposed that the government be given the power to apply any
economic measures necessary to participate in collective action.
The 1934 Labour Party Conference and the Trades Union Congress overwhelmingly approved this statement, a stand which was
reiterated in 1935 on the eve of the Italian invasion. Most Englishmen harboring pro-League, anti-Fascist, and anti-Nazi sentiments
joined in Labour's foreign policy.[46]

Labour never squarely met the question of military sanctions
for the defense of collective security. In Parliament, Labour members consistently voted against the service estimates, though, as
Attlee pointed out, their stand was not against arms per se, but
against the level of armaments the government proposed. Yet Conservatives continually contrasted the Labour demand for strong
British leadership with Labour's negative vote on armaments. Labour thought that economic sanctions wholeheartedly supported
by Great Britain and the League would deter or defeat an aggressor, and thus avoid the potentially embarrassing question of the
use of military force.[47]

The first full-scale debate on the government's policy toward the
Italo-Ethiopian crisis clearly demonstrated the attitudes of the
British parties. In the House of Commons on June 5, the Liberal
and Labour opposition demanded a clear and definitive statement
by the government of British determination to support the League
Covenant. In addition, Attlee urged the government to warn Mussolini that in case of aggressive action Britain would deny Italy the
use of the Suez Canal.

Speaking for the right-wing Conservatives, Lieutenant Colonel
Sir Arnold Wilson expressed "alarm" at the words of Attlee and
other opposition speakers. He feared any such widespread British

commitment as a world policeman and thought closure of the Suez Canal tantamount to a declaration of war. Anthony Eden, in his new position as Minister for League of Nations Affairs, agreed with Attlee on the value of the League but argued that the opposition had overlooked the important role already played by the League in the Italo-Ethiopian dispute. Eden assured the House that the government would not cease exerting itself to promote a peaceful settlement, but added that there was no reason why British and Italian interests could not develop harmoniously side by side.[48]

The Peace Ballot, dramatic evidence of an aroused public opinion, spurred the Conservative government to action in the Italo-Ethiopian dispute. The results of this national referendum were released in June 1935, though the trend was known earlier. The League of Nations Union had initiated the Peace Ballot in 1934 as an effort to demonstrate continued British support for the League, despite its failure in the Manchurian crisis and the collapse of the Geneva Disarmament Conference. A National Declaration Committee composed of representatives of 38 organizations, including the Liberal and Labour parties, carried out the huge poll. The ruling Conservatives refused to participate in it, alleging that the Peace Ballot was pacifistic, idealistic, and misleadingly simplified. They doubted the competence of most voters to make a serious judgment on the real issues. Nevertheless, many Conservatives did participate as individuals through the League of Nations Union, led by Robert Cecil, a Conservative lord.[49]

Over eleven and one-half million people voted in the plebiscite, which overwhelmingly endorsed British membership in the League of Nations, reduction in armaments by international agreement, and collective security by economic and even military measures. The question of using armed force in the support of collective security brought the closest vote: 60 per cent in favor, 20 per cent opposed, and 20 per cent abstaining. The announcement of these results coincided with increasing public concern over Italian intentions in Ethiopia and probably had a decisive influence on government policy.[50]

Many in France and Italy, and even in the United States, firmly believed that imperial interests in the Red Sea and the Nile basin dictated the concern shown by British public opinion. They viewed cynically the facile manner in which Great Britain appeared to combine idealism and self-interest in its foreign policy. This view, however, was without foundation. The empire-loving right wing distrusted the League of Nations and collective security, and tended to sympathize genuinely with Italian aspirations. At the same time a majority of the anticolonialist Labour party demanded a stronger stand against Italy. Only in the larger sense that world peace and the rule of law were in the best interests of Great Britain, the Commonwealth, and the Empire could one consider British public opinion self-interested.[51]

In the light of the intransigence of public opinion, Eden informed Aloisi that the cabinet had instructed him to return to London with proof that the League of Nations was handling the dispute.[52] After lengthy negotiation by Eden, the League Council secured a compromise agreement on May 25 by which Italy once again promised to pursue the terms of the 1928 Friendship Treaty with Ethiopia. If by July 25 the four-man arbitration commission (two men designated by each country) had not agreed upon a solution to the dispute or upon the selection of the fifth arbitrator, or if by August 25 the commission had not completed the whole procedure of arbitration and reached a final settlement, the Council would then without further delay consider the entire Italo-Ethiopian conflict.

Eden later boasted that the leadership exerted by the British government had secured the Council resolution and established the timetable.[53] He neglected to add that the Council at the same time had completely ignored Haile Selassie's urgent appeal for a halt to Italian military preparations on Ethiopia's northern and southeastern frontiers. Aloisi and the "half-Fascists" of the Italian Foreign Office in Rome could accept the Council resolution because it neither compromised the Italian position nor forced Italy to withdraw from Geneva. Mussolini's fury about British press reports of a diplomatic victory gradually abated.[54]

During the summer of 1935 the British made several determined efforts to achieve a compromise solution of the Italo-Ethiopian dispute. In an effort to escape its dilemma, the government sent Eden to Rome in late June on a personal mission to Il Duce. He was ostensibly to explain to Mussolini the recently concluded Anglo-German Naval Agreement, which appeared to represent British acceptance of Hitler's unilateral repudiation of Part Five

of the Versailles Treaty. More important, however, Eden intended
to present proposals for a peaceful solution of the Italo-Ethiopian
dispute. A personal mission was chosen, in preference to diplomatic channels, to underline the concern of the British government with the dispute. In addition, it was questionable whether
Mussolini ever learned the real views of the outside world from his
diplomatic envoys.[55]

As Eden subsequently explained, he emphasized to Mussolini
that British foreign policy loyally supported the League of Nations
and that Great Britain could not remain indifferent to events that
might profoundly affect the League's future. Therefore, the government had studied anxiously whether it could make any con-
structive contribution to the promotion of a solution. "The purpose of the offer," Eden stated, "was to obtain a final settlement of
the dispute between Italy and Abyssinia. The object was to give
some *quid pro quo* to Abyssinia for territorial and economic concessions by her which the settlement of the dispute with Italy might
entail." By territorial concessions Eden meant cession of part of
the Ogaden steppe to Italy in return for an Ethiopian seaport at
Zeila in British Somaliland. By economic concessions he meant
the selection of Italian advisers by Haile Selassie and the settlement of Italians in part of Ethiopia.[56]

Mussolini, Aloisi wrote in his diary, "poured cold water" on
Eden's offer, frankly informing him that Italy demanded direct
occupation of the non-Amharic territories and supervision over
the rest. Eden's proposals were totally rejected by Mussolini as
insufficient. The otherwise moderate Guariglia and Aloisi thought
Eden's plan an insult to the Italian people, and in fact a trap,
which would give predominance in Ethiopia to Great Britain and
only a desert to Italy. On the other hand, Mussolini's minimum
demands, which varied little from those related to Eden, always
amounted to more than British public opinion could accept. Following Eden's personal mission to Rome, the Anglo-Italian disagreement came into the open, a result opposite to that the British
had hoped for. The British government had sunk even deeper in
its dilemma.[57]

After six months of procrastination, Italy and Ethiopia finally
constituted an arbitration commission to investigate the Wal-Wal
incident. After examining the dispute briefly, however, it broke

up on July 9 because of disagreement on jurisdiction and terms of reference. Ethiopia demanded the consideration of boundary lines since the location of Wal-Wal within Ethiopian territory composed the heart of its case. Italy required, on the other hand, that only the specific incident be arbitrated. Since the two sides could not agree on the basis for arbitration, Italy refused to designate the fifth arbitrator.

The League Council, therefore, met on July 31, 1935, according to the timetable established in May. Laval and Eden dutifully produced what they referred to as a compromise, by which Italy agreed to name the fifth arbitrator while Ethiopia acquiesced in abandoning the boundary question. In addition, Italy dropped objections to negotiations outside the League of Nations by the signatories of the Tripartite Treaty of 1906. Italy agreed to this procedure not because of any desire for a compromise solution, but once again merely to gain time and to keep the issue from the Council agenda.[58]

Great Britain and France, however, took seriously the tripartite negotiations in Paris on August 16–19. They made a determined effort to compromise with Mussolini. Under strict instructions, Aloisi refused to cooperate. Mussolini had instructed his representative to act more as a fighter than a diplomat, a Fascist than a negotiator: "I want no agreement unless they can concede everything including the beheading of the Emperor. . . . What we seek is to gain time."[59]

Between them, Laval and Eden evolved a compromise plan that would meet Italy's genuine grievances and provide substantial economic advantages while at the same time maintain Ethiopian sovereignty and League prestige. This plan provided for the reorganization of Ethiopia by advisers from many foreign countries, extensive economic privileges to Italy (including the right to build a railroad between Italian Somaliland and Eritrea), and cession to Italy of part of the Tigrai and Ogaden provinces in exchange for an Ethiopian outlet to the sea. Mussolini rejected the plan outright.[60]

The collapse of the Paris conversations discouraged the British. Foreign Secretary Hoare thought nothing could stop Italian military action in Ethiopia, and Eden felt that Britain had spared no efforts or means. Hoare told the America Chargé, Ray Atherton, that England would now have to consider its position. Atherton summarized his own assessment of developments for the State Department: "There is a growing conviction here that Mussolini is not bluffing and that if measures which interfere with his Abyssinian policy are undertaken, England may be put in a position where she must either take action alone against Italy or accept a passive role temporarily." Great Britain, Atherton concluded, might urge a strong policy at Geneva, but could take direct action only in conjunction with France, and only to such an extent as France could be persuaded to accept.[61]

Shortly thereafter, the Italo-Ethiopian Arbitration Commission reached the ambiguous but politic decision that Italy had no reason to precipitate the incident and that it could not prove the fault of Ethiopia. The Wal-Wal incident, apparently settled after a nine-months delay, had never been anything more than a blind behind which Italy prepared for military conquest.

Chapter Two

American Foreign Policy and the Italo-Ethiopian Dispute

During the two decades between the First and Second World Wars, Americans were engaged in a crucial debate on the role of the United States in international affairs. The conflict raged between adherents to the nineteeth-century tradition of political isolation and advocates of the twentieth-century concepts of international-ism and collective security. The central issues of the debate, in which the isolationists won every point but the last one, were focused on opposite views of how best to guarantee American se-curity and how much responsibility the United States had for maintaining world peace.

While isolationists and internationalists agreed upon keeping the United States out of war, they had different policies for achiev-ing this goal. Isolationists scoffed at their opponents' hope of set-tling quarrels and preventing wars by cooperation among nations. They opposed any policy that might involve the United States in foreign political obligations. Isolationists did not shun all contact with the rest of the world, but they saw external political commit-ments as invariably leading to entangling alliances. The best way to avoid war, they thought, was to reduce American participation in foreign political affairs.[1]

Internationalists, on the other hand, argued that the United States, which had emerged from the First World War as the strong-est and wealthiest nation in an increasingly interdependent world, could no longer escape the effects of foreign problems. They insisted that sooner or later such problems would threaten American security and self-interest. The United States, they said, should cooperate with other nations to prevent disputes from exploding into armed conflict; the best way to avoid a war was to keep it from starting. As Secretary of State Cordell Hull reminded isolationists, even the allegedly stupid and blundering United States could not get involved in a war if all wars were prevented.[2]

Isolationism appealed to various people for various reasons. One important factor was ethnic. German- and Irish-Americans remembered that intervention in the First World War had aided Great Britain, and opposed an active policy after the war on the ground that it would involve cooperation with the hated British. During the Italo-Ethiopian War Italian-Americans joined them, fearing that American involvement would hurt Italy.[3]

A second source of isolationism was socio-economic. Conservatives such as Senator Arthur H. Vandenberg of Michigan worried that an activist foreign policy might disturb the status quo at home. Liberals such as Senator George W. Norris of Nebraska feared that an internationalist foreign policy might restrict domestic reform or believed that selfish economic interests promoted wars.

Isolationists might be inclined toward pacifism, like Senators Norris and Gerald P. Nye of North Dakota, or toward nationalism, like Senators William E. Borah of Idaho and Hiram Johnson of California. The pacifists, characterized as favoring peace at any price, advocated the surrender of neutral rights and foreign trade, if necessary, to keep the United States from war. (Representing agricultural areas, they could easily make this sacrifice.) The nationalists, on the other hand, argued that the government could best protect American interests and escape Europe's inevitable wars by insisting on the traditional rights of neutrals to trade freely with anyone anywhere. Disagreement between these two varieties of isolationism was a prime cause of the impasse in early 1936 over a permanent neutrality law.[4]

Moderate and liberal isolationists found especially attractive such peace organizations as the National Council for the Prevention of War, the Women's International League for Peace and Freedom, and the Fellowship of Reconciliation, groups that stressed pacifism, disarmament, and the outlawing of war. Such organizations were opposed not to international consultation itself, but to political or military obligations that might arise from it. They distinguished between consultation to remove the causes of war and positive action to enforce peace through sanctions or coercion.

Internationalism, which appealed particularly to the educated and professional classes and to Americans of British descent, centered in the more conservative, better-established, and more adequately financed peace organizations such as the League of Nations Association, the World Peace Foundation, and the Carnegie Endowment for International Peace. Such groups believed that international consultation could be meaningful only when some degree of collective security had been established, and urged that America commit itself to the preservation of peace. At a minimum, internationalists thought, the United States must indicate that it would not frustrate the activities of other nations in punishing an aggressor.[5]

A return to what President Warren G. Harding termed "normalcy" was inevitable at the close of the First World War. But the idealistic hopes that wartime President Woodrow Wilson had encouraged in Americans increased this reaction. The swing back to the traditional American foreign policy of political isolation was accelerated by disillusionment with the peace settlement on the part of liberals and disappointed ethnic groups, by general relief at the end of the war and its vexatious regulations, and by the Senate's rejection of the Treaty of Versailles, including the Covenant of the League of Nations.

The United States deliberately withdrew from the political affairs of the world. The League of Nations became a hot potato in domestic politics. For the first six months in 1921, the Harding administration left communications from the League unanswered; thereafter, it sent replies unsigned in the third person and delivered them through American diplomatic channels in Switzerland. Beginning in 1923, as American xenophobia subsided, the United States gradually and cautiously participated, first with observers and later with official delegates, in nonpolitical and humanitarian conferences sponsored by the League of Nations. Relations had so improved during the late 1920's that an American observer sat with the League Council in 1931 in considering the Manchurian crisis.[6]

But if isolationism had appeared to subside during the relative economic prosperity of the 1920's, when the League of Nations seemed a useful and successful organization, the next decade reversed the trend. The impact of the depression slashed international economic ties, brought the repudiation of war debts, and spurred economic nationalism in America as in other nations. A new wave of aggression spread over the world, and Americans began to fear another war.[7]

America's increasingly strong isolationist sentiment in the 1930's made cooperation with other nations in settling disputes difficult if not impossible. Franklin D. Roosevelt's administration, which often differed with the powerful senatorial isolationists, had to plan its programs cautiously to avoid an open and perhaps disastrous clash on foreign policy.

Like Hull, Roosevelt was an ardent Wilsonian. As Assistant Secretary of the Navy under President Wilson and as the Democratic vice-presidential nominee in 1920, he had enthusiastically supported the League of Nations. When he became President himself in 1933, Roosevelt was still essentially sympathetic to the world organization, but he understood that domestic political considerations prevented the United States from joining it. In seeking the Democratic presidential nomination in 1932, Roosevelt had promised the isolationist newspaper publisher William Randolph Hearst that the United States would not join the League of Nations. Yet his true attitude toward the League was illustrated in an address on December 28, 1933, to the Woodrow Wilson Foundation. The League, said the President, has rendered important services from assistance to health and commerce to settlement of a great many disputes. "Today the United States is cooperating openly in the fuller utilization of the League of Nations machinery than ever before. . . . We are giving cooperation to the League in every matter which is not primarily political."[8]

During Roosevelt's first term, domestic policy took clear precedence over foreign policy because of the serious economic depression at home. The President was reluctant to raise any issue that might arouse the wrath of the Senate's powerful isolationists, especially the liberals, whose support he wanted for the domestic measures of his New Deal. Roosevelt's foreign policy gyrated erratically, the pragmatic by-product of what the domestic political conditions of the moment required.[9]

The President torpedoed the London Economic Conference in 1933 because of his nationalist economic policies. He considered sending an ambassador to the League but dropped the idea for fear of isolationist fury. Secretary of Labor Frances Perkins had only the most minimal presidential support in her shrewd and successful effort to obtain Senate approval of American membership in the International Labor Organization.[10]

On the other hand, Roosevelt invigorated the "good neighbor policy" initiated by his Republican predecessor, and encouraged Secretary Hull's enthusiastic work for the reciprocal trade program. Of particular importance, he authorized the American representative to the Geneva Disarmament Conference in 1933, Norman Davis, to promise that if a disarmament agreement were achieved, the United States would not obstruct the action of other nations in implementing collective security measures against an aggressor. Moreover, contrary to his political judgment, Roosevelt yielded to Hull's pleas and called for American adherence to the World Court.[11]

The battle over the World Court demonstrated the complexity of the problems the President faced in securing Congressional approval of his foreign policies. Because it occurred in January 1935 at the start of the Italo-Ethiopian crisis, the World Court episode is of particular interest. Previous presidents had advocated American membership, though not without stringent reservations. The 1932 platforms of both major political parties had endorsed it. After Roosevelt yielded to Hull's urging, he informed William Dodd, the United States Ambassador to Germany, that he would recommend approval but that he was skeptical of American public opinion.[12] On January 16, in a special message to the Senate, Roosevelt proposed that the United States "throw its weight into the scale in favor of peace" by adhering to the World Court.

The violent charges of isolationists and a spectacular last-minute attack by Father Coughlin and the Hearst press helped defeat the resolution, even though it had required only that the United States pay a small share of the World Court's annual expenses.[13] Some of Roosevelt's friends, such as the internationalist Dodd, thought the President might have exerted his authority to a greater extent, while others, such as Secretary of the Interior Harold L. Ickes, could not understand why he had ever involved himself so deeply in such a controversial issue. Although Roosevelt had waged only a half-hearted struggle against the determined isolationists, he was active enough to make them distrust him in foreign affairs, and they wished to tie his hands in the future.[14]

The idea of an embargo on the shipment of arms to belligerent countries had been discussed intermittently for a decade before the Italo-Ethiopian crisis.[15] Should this arms embargo be mandatory or at the President's discretion, and should it apply to both belligerents or only to the aggressor? The increasing tensions in Europe during 1935 and the threat of war between Italy and Ethiopia led both Congress and the public to demand a definite neutrality policy.

Americans agreed almost unanimously that the country should not intervene in the approaching Italo-Ethiopian War. The only genuine difference of opinion between internationalists and isolationists pertained to the kind of neutrality legislation to be enacted. Internationalists, centered in the State Department, in conservative peace organizations such as the League of Nations Association and the World Peace Foundation, and in influential newspapers such as the *New York Times,* urged American neutrality within a framework of cooperation with the League of Nations or consultation by means of the Kellogg-Briand Pact. A discretionary embargo would permit the United States to cooperate in efforts by other governments or the League of Nations to blockade any state that violated treaties. Not only would a discretionary embargo warn a potential aggressor not to expect material assistance from the United States, but also it would reassure other governments that the United States would not frustrate their efforts to thwart aggression.

Isolationists, by contrast, who were strongly represented in the Senate, feared that discretion in the hands of an internationalist President might result in just the kind of unneutral behavior that they alleged had pushed the United States into war in 1917. They accordingly demanded a neutrality law that would compel the President to proclaim a mandatory embargo on both belligerents.

The sensational activities and oversimplified allegations of the Senate Committee Investigating the Munitions Industry greatly strengthened the isolationist position during 1935. This Commit-

tee, better known as the Nye Committee after its chairman, Senator Gerald P. Nye, was established in 1934 to investigate the munitions industry; it charged that financiers and munitions makers
had pushed a reluctant United States into the First World War.
This accusation and the increasing threat during 1935 of war in
East Africa combined to arouse a powerful demand for neutrality
legislation to prevent the United States from repeating the "mis-
takes of 1914–1917." Just at the moment when American influence
might have lessened the threat of war abroad, the well-publicized
revelations of the Nye Committee threw the United States even
further into isolationism. Secretary Hull remarked in his memoirs
that it was doubtful if any Congressional committee had ever had
a more unfortunate effect on the conduct of American foreign relations.[16]

The State Department and isolationists in the Senate sparred
until August 1935. The Department sought to persuade the Senate
Foreign Relations Committee that mandatory embargo legislation
could not pass the House of Representatives: it was presidential
discretion or nothing.[17] For a while this argument checked the am-
bitious plans of the Nye Committee, but it did not persuade the
Senate to approve presidential discretion. Secretary Hull opposed
any neutrality legislation without a flexible provision, especially
"legislation which, by telling the world what we would not do in
case of war, would prevent our exercising our influence to prevent
war; nor legislation, which if war came, would preclude our render-
ing the least assistance to the world organization, the League of
Nations, in its efforts to bring the war to an end."[18]

But President Roosevelt hesitated to make a stand. When the
crucial time arrived in late summer, Hull failed to secure the
President's active backing for discretionary neutrality legislation.
At a press conference on July 24, Roosevelt stated ambiguously
that he did favor neutrality legislation in the event of a conflict
but feared that consideration of a bill might unduly prolong the
current session of Congress. In response to a question, he refused
to be specific, merely stating with a smile that some features of a
neutrality bill might provide for discretion and others not.[19]

Roosevelt understood the drift of events abroad and personally
favored a discretionary embargo, which would maintain executive
control over foreign policy and permit international cooperation

against an aggressor. But there was an important domestic program to put through Congress, as well as a political party to lead
in the 1936 elections. In moving from the first to the second New
Deal during 1935, Roosevelt wanted the aid of liberal isolationists
such as Senators Nye, Borah, and Norris.[20] The World Court
struggle earlier in the year had clearly shown the sentiment these
isolationists could arouse and the power they could wield. The
stories of the President's decreasing popularity during 1935, par-
tially substantiated by off-year election losses, argued further for
caution in foreign policy. At the same time, reports from American
diplomats abroad suggested that even a legislative victory might be
worthless because of the apparently halfhearted efforts of Great
Britain and France to safeguard Ethiopia.[21]

In late July the State Department had forwarded its draft neutrality bill to the House Foreign Affairs and Senate Foreign Relations Committees. The isolationists were particularly strong on the
latter, a subcommittee of which on August 7 rejected the Department's recommendation for discretionary provisions.[22] On August
19, as Congress met to pass a last flurry of bills before adjournment,
Hull urged Roosevelt to make a final effort to secure enactment of
a discretionary arms embargo resolution. Hull's draft resolution,
noting the possibility of war between Italy and Ethiopia, authorized the President at his discretion to place an embargo on arms,
ammunition, and implements of war unless or until ordered otherwise by Congress. The resolution proposed by Hull would termi-
nate 30 days after the convening of the next session of Congress
and would thus be a mere stopgap measure, applying only to the
Italo-Ethiopian dispute.[23]

Roosevelt signed Hull's draft letter to Senator Key Pittman,
Chairman of the Senate Foreign Relations Committee, who was
sympathetic to the isolationist viewpoint.[24] The President added
in his own handwriting, "I hope you will note that as drawn this
is only a temporary emergency act to cover the recess period of
Congress." Before the letter was sent, however, Stephen Early,
Roosevelt's secretary, telephoned Pittman, who informed him that
the Senate Foreign Relations Committee had refused to approve
the discretionary embargo and had insisted on applying any embargo to both belligerents. "I tell you, Steve," exclaimed Pittman,
"the President is riding for a fall if he insists on designating the

aggressor in accordance with the League of Nations." If Roosevelt wanted the bill introduced, Pittman agreed to do so without comment but warned that "he will be licked as sure as hell." The White House did not send Hull's letter to Pittman.[25]

The Senate Foreign Relations Committee agreed on the same day, August 19, that it would report some kind of neutrality legislation before the session ended. Pittman thereupon introduced his own neutrality resolution combining the arms registration articles of the State Department draft with a nondiscretionary embargo provision. At the same time, isolationists led by Senators Nye and Bennett Clark increased the pressure on both Pittman and the administration by warning that the Italo-Ethiopian crisis might lead to war. They threatened a long filibuster if the Senate did not consider a neutrality resolution ahead of the administration's Guffey Coal Bill.[26]

On August 21 the Senate passed the Pittman resolution. That evening Roosevelt, Hull, Assistant Secretary of State R. Walton Moore, and Sam D. McReynolds, Chairman of the House Foreign Affairs Committee, met at the White House to consider possible modifications of the resolution. With the Senate adamant in opposing a discretionary embargo, and numerous Congressmen demanding some kind of neutrality legislation in the face of an Italo-Ethiopian War, the President reluctantly proposed a compromise to accept the Pittman resolution for a period of six months.[27] This satisfied no one, and both isolationists and internationalists began preparing for a second round when Congress would reconvene in January.

Hull informed Roosevelt that despite his strong objections to the joint resolution, he did not feel "under the circumstances" that he could advise the President to reject it. A veto might provoke an open conflict with Congress that would end disastrously for the administration. The Secretary objected most strenuously to the mandatory feature of the embargo as "an invasion of the constitutional and traditional power of the Executive to conduct the foreign relations of the United States," and as an action that would "tend to deprive this Government of a great measure of its influence in promoting and preserving peace." Hull was concerned both with the question of who made American foreign policy—Congress or the Executive—and with the attitude the United States would take in support of collective action against an aggressor.[28]

In a statement released on August 31 when he signed the joint resolution, Roosevelt reiterated the intention of the United States to avoid any action that might involve the country in war. He objected, however, to the inflexible provisions of the embargo on arms, ammunition, and implements of war, arguing that neither Congress nor the President could foresee all future situations. Although he signed the resolution, Roosevelt insisted on the need for further consideration of neutrality legislation. He assured reporters, however, that the measure met the "needs of the existing situation."[29]

The "circumstances" to which Hull had alluded in his August 29 letter, and the "needs of the existing situation" noted by Roosevelt, referred to the fact that the nondiscretionary embargo would last only six months. In the only conflict on the horizon, such an arms embargo would be harder on the Italian aggressor than on the Ethiopian victim. In case of action by the League of Nations, both the League countries and the United States would deny arms to Italy, while Ethiopia might still secure supplies from the League members. Internationalists hoped that they could persuade public opinion and Congress to support a discretionary embargo when the legislative body reconvened in January.[30]

Chapter Three

The United States and Ethiopia

Most Americans knew nothing of Ethiopia when the Italo-Ethiopian crisis began in December 1934 with the clash at Wal-Wal. Although the United States maintained one of the eight foreign legations in the Ethiopian capital of Addis Ababa, Americans had little interest in the ancient and proud Christian empire. Missionary and philanthropic activities engaged most of the hundred or so American citizens living in the country on the eve of the struggle with Italy. Annual trade between Ethiopia and the United States amounted to less than half a million dollars. The only noteworthy American commercial interests were the Singer Sewing Machine Company and the J. G. White Engineering Corporation. The latter, a New York City firm, had completed several surveys of Lake Tana and awaited a contract for building a dam there.[1]

The United States had no political or material interest in Ethiopia. It maintained a legation in Addis Ababa primarily "to satisfy the apparently eager wish of the Emperor" for American representation.[2] Because Haile Selassie was suspicious of the European nations whose colonies surrounded Ethiopia, he especially desired diplomatic representation from a disinterested power like the United States. Despite British resentment, the Emperor had selected an American engineering firm to survey Lake Tana, and had chosen an American, Everett Colson, as his principal diplomatic and financial adviser. The Emperor explained to the new American Chargé d'Affaires, W. Perry George, a month before the incident at Wal-Wal, that he had "worked very hard to secure American diplomatic representation in Ethiopia. We cherish our relations with the United States, understanding that their friendly character is undisturbed by any political aims in this part of the world, and realizing our great need for politically disinterested cooperation in our economic development."[3]

The American Military Attaché in Rome advised the War Department continually during the latter half of 1934 that the Italian government was preparing for the conquest of Ethiopia. Offensive operations would commence whenever Ethiopia committed an "overt act."[4] On September 22 Ambassador William C. Bullitt in Moscow telegraphed the State Department that he had learned from his Italian colleague that Britain and France had promised not to interfere in any way with Italian ambitions in Ethiopia. The Italian Ambassador had assured Bullitt that Ethiopia could expect no outside aid and would soon be forced to "acquiesce in the reasonable demands of Italy."[5]

Under Secretary William Phillips immediately notified American representatives in the European and Ethiopian capitals of these reports.[6] In response to queries, the French admitted that Italy desired a free hand in Ethiopia, but officials in Paris refused to indicate their government's response. The British indignantly denied they had acquiesced in Italy's plans. And the Italians insisted they had sent military supplies to Italian Somaliland and Eritrea only for defensive purposes. According to Chargé George in Addis Ababa, reporting his conversation with the Italian Minister, "it was noticeable that the adverb of time occasionally crept into the conversation."[7]

Forewarned by these rumors, the State Department was not completely surprised by the Wal-Wal incident. Wallace Murray, Chief of the Division of Near Eastern Affairs, saw little reason to doubt that Italy had received a free hand in Ethiopia, at least from France and possibly from Great Britain. In any case, he did not think either country would actively oppose Mussolini's ambitions because of the need for Italian cooperation in Europe. Sooner or later, Murray realized, someone would move to invoke the Kellogg-Briand Pact, which had been co-sponsored by the United States. "We ought to leave such invocation to the League of Nations and

make every effort to avoid having the matter dumped in our lap,"
he pointed out. "Both Ethiopia and Italy are members of the
League of Nations and it seems to me that Geneva is the proper
forum where matters of this nature should be aired and settled."
Murray's assistant, Philip H. Alling, agreed that if the Kellogg-
Briand Pact were to be invoked, the League of Nations should invoke it, particularly "in the case of the present Italian-Ethiopian
dispute with which the United States is not even remotely concerned." The State Department obviously had no wish to become
involved in what bore the appearance of another colonial arrangement among Britain, France, and Italy.[8]

On the evening of December 18 Haile Selassie called George to
a private audience. The Emperor assured George that he was not
seeking American mediation but that his country would welcome
some gesture from the United States in support of a peaceful settlement of the Italo-Ethiopian clash. He insisted that Ethiopia would
accede to no demand without arbitration, and if menaced by Italy
would fight for its frontiers.[9] It was logical for him to appeal to
the United States, which had reminded China and Russia in 1929
and Japan in 1931 of their obligations as signatories to the Kellogg-
Briand Pact.

In line with the policy advised by the Division of Near Eastern
Affairs, George assured the Emperor that the United States government believed the unfortunate incident at Wal-Wal susceptible of
settlement by peaceful means, hopefully by Italy and Ethiopia
alone. As for a gesture by the United States, since Ethiopia had
brought the incident to the attention of the League of Nations, the
United States did not think it could properly take any action.[10]
This polite but empty American response must have disappointed
the Emperor, who undoubtedly feared exactly what the State Department expected.

Six months later, disillusioned with the League of Nations, which
appeared to be more concerned with mollifying Italy than with
protecting Ethiopia, Haile Selassie tried again to secure American
assistance. On the evening of July 3, 1935, he called George to the
Palace. After carefully recapitulating events since the Wal-Wal
clash of the previous December, he reminded George of Ethiopia's
appeal to the United States at that time. The Emperor pointed out

that since Anthony Eden's fruitless mission to Rome in late June, no one could doubt the Italian goal of military conquest. Insisting that his country would continue to cooperate with the League of Nations, Haile Selassie formally requested the American government "to examine means of securing Italy's observance of engagements as signatory of the Kellogg Pact."*

Hull replied immediately, even before the full text of Haile Selassie's appeal had arrived from Addis Ababa. (Since Hull had indicated that he would respond only after receiving the full text, it was probably Roosevelt who directed that it be sent immediately, and who penciled in a few changes to strengthen Hull's cautious draft.) Hull's reply noted the American interest in maintaining world peace and his government's gratification that the League had given its attention to the Italo-Ethiopian controversy now in the process of arbitration. "Furthermore, and *of great importance, in view of the provisions of the Pact of Paris, to which both Italy and Ethiopia* [pencil changes] are parties, in common with sixty-one other countries, my Government would be loath to believe that either of them would resort to other than pacific means as a method of dealing with this controversy or would permit any situation to arise which would be inconsistent with the commitments of the Pact."[11]

George received the reply on the afternoon of July 6 and obtained an immediate audience with the Emperor, who was highly agitated and obviously impatient to know the contents of the Department's reply. The Emperor listened to George's translation into French; then he "remained silent for some minutes in deep thought." He asked "me to render the closing paragraph once more, slowly," George reported. "He then seemed relieved and pleased, thanked me, and asked a number of questions regarding the Kellogg Pact."[12]

Roosevelt and Hull had had three aims in mind in formulating their reply: to remind all parties, particularly Italy and Ethiopia, of the terms of the Pact; to avoid placing the United States in a potentially embarrassing position as the initiator of any action;

---

* George suggested that the Emperor had deliberately selected the eve of the Fourth of July as the most appropriate moment to appeal to the United States for the invocation of the Kellogg-Briand Pact. (George to Hull, July 4 and 15, 1935.)

and to protect the Pact itself from such open defiance as Japan had accomplished in the Manchurian crisis. The steady stream of intelligence from American diplomats reporting Anglo-French indecisiveness gave little encouragement for the administration to brave isolationist wrath. Hull was so pessimistic that on July 2 the State Department advised Americans in Ethiopia to leave the country. (Most, being missionaries, ignored this advice, contending that they served a higher Power and that their medical services would prove extremely useful to Ethiopia in its hour of need.) The State Department seemed to be primarily concerned with reducing American interests and responsibilities in this crisis so as to avoid possible incidents.[13]

To the amazement of Roosevelt and Hull, Haile Selassie interpreted their cautious reply as tantamount to a United States rejection of the Kellogg-Briand Pact. Worse than this, they were appalled to learn of Italian approval of their response. The Associated Press reported from Rome on July 7 that "Washington's answer to Emperor Haile Selassie's request for invocation of the Briand-Kellogg Pact was held before the Italian public as evidence of the United States' friendliness toward Italy and an American realization that this country is justified in its stand."[14]

The confusion caused by the administration's caution now forced it to resolute action. On July 10 Hull informed the Italian Ambassador, Augusto Rosso, that the misinterpretation of his response to the Emperor had greatly surprised him. Far from being disinterested, Hull said his government was increasingly concerned with the serious situation arising from the dispute and earnestly hoped for a peaceful solution.[15]

The following day Hull notified the British and French ambassadors of exactly what he had said to their Italian colleague. Instead of mentioning the Associated Press dispatch from Rome, however, which had caused him to speak to Rosso, Hull referred the two ambassadors to an article in the *Boston Transcript* from its London correspondent. According to this article, the British public almost unanimously regarded the Kellogg-Briand Pact as dead, owing to the "brusque refusal of the American Government to invoke that Pact to prevent the Italo-Ethiopian conflict from developing into an open war."[16]

When press and diplomatic opinion throughout the world, including the United States, continued to take this view, Hull issued an entirely new statement on July 12. He insisted that the "Pact of Paris is no less binding now than when it was entered into by the sixty-three nations that are parties to it." It is, he continued, "an agreement and a solemn obligation that the settlement or solution of all disputes or conflicts among nations of whatever nature or of whatever origin shall never be sought except by pacific means. The United States and other nations are interested in the maintenance of the Pact and the sanctity of the international commitments assumed thereby for the promotion and maintenance of peace among the nations of the world."[17] The *New York Times,* which had headlined the initial response to the Ethiopian Emperor as "President Rejects Ethiopia's Appeal for Peace Effort," hailed the second statement as a "sweeping declaration in support of the Kellogg-Briand Pact" that stopped only "slightly short" of granting Haile Selassie's original appeal. Thus, because of the interpretation that the press—especially the controlled Italian press—had placed on the initial American reply, Haile Selassie virtually achieved his goal of an American invocation of the Kellogg-Briand Pact.

But, to be effective, it seemed clear that American assistance would have to go further than mere moral exhortation. The Washington correspondent of *The Times* (London) noted that Hull's statements did not indicate any intention on the part of the United States "to leave the lofty heights of exposition and admonition for the more dangerous fields of active participation in efforts to compose the Italo-Ethiopian quarrel."[18]

Haile Selassie's next move was a curious one. On August 29 he granted an extensive 75-year mineral concession to a British adventurer, Francis W. Rickett, who had negotiated a lease for the African Exploration and Development Corporation. This exclusive grant covered half of Ethiopia, including all of its eastern and southeastern territory bordering on Italian Somaliland and Eritrea. Italy had long considered this area within its sphere of influence. Anglo-American oil interests, it was rumored, lay behind the deal.[19]

The news of this far-reaching concession horrified London and Washington. The British thought the action "truly deplorable" because it appeared to make them hypocritical—denouncing Italian ambitions while plotting their own imperialist deal. The Foreign Office instructed the British Minister in Addis Ababa to urge the Emperor to withhold the grant. In a press release denying any knowledge of it as well as any support for Rickett, the British government pointed out that except for Lake Tana, Great Britain had no economic interest in Ethiopia. The government stressed that in its earnest desire to take no step that might aggravate the Italo-Ethiopian controversy, it had made no decision on an Ethiopian offer of May 1935 to conclude an agreement for a dam at Lake Tana.[20]

Hull also disclaimed knowledge of the strange concession. He declared that the American government could not oversee American business interests abroad, and that it took an interest only when American citizens received unfair treatment. Plainly annoyed that he knew nothing about the Ethiopian concession, Hull could only decline responsibility.[21]

Seeking to unravel the mystery, the State Department checked a report from Cornelius Van H. Engert, who had replaced George as American Chargé in Addis Ababa in July, that the African Exploration and Development Corporation was registered in Delaware and had connections with Standard Oil. Officials could discover only that Delaware law did not require registering corporations to indicate whether they were independent firms or subsidiaries of larger organizations. They could not contact Standard Oil, since company offices closed on Saturdays during the summer. But Sunday-morning readers of the *New York Times* learned that the African Exploration and Development Corporation had been registered on July 11 by the United States Corporation Company, a skeleton company that specialized in incorporating projects for interests wanting to remain temporarily behind the scenes. In addition, officials of all Standard Oil companies denied knowledge of the Rickett concession. The mystery increased over the long Labor Day weekend.[22]

Meanwhile in Addis Ababa, Rickett and the Emperor's financial adviser, Colson, declared that the concession involved entirely American capital. The voluble Rickett admitted that negotiations for an oil concession had begun early in January and had been concluded rapidly during the summer, in order to give Italy second thoughts about an attack. After the failure of the Paris negotiations among Great Britain, France, and Italy in mid-August, Haile Selassie had called Rickett to Addis Ababa. Five days of secret negotiations followed—so secret, it was reported, that Rickett and the other negotiators had entered and left by a hidden back door and the Ethiopian translators had received separate pages to transcribe.[23]

Haile Selassie admitted that the concession involved only the United States—and deliberately so. He indignantly asked what right Great Britain had to advise withdrawal of the grant or to object that it violated the Tripartite Treaty of 1906. The Emperor pointed out that a sovereign state could do as it pleased with its own territory, and that neither Ethiopia nor the United States had signed the Treaty. Indeed, Haile Selassie concluded, "That is one of the reasons I gave the concession to Standard Oil."[24]

The story rapidly unfolded in Washington on Tuesday, September 3. Hull held a noon press conference at which he indicated that the government still lacked the information it needed, and repeated that the United States could not assume responsibility for safeguarding private ventures. Even as Hull spoke, however, two officials of the Standard Vacuum Oil Company called voluntarily at the State Department to discuss the case. Chairman of the Board George S. Walden and Vice President Henry Dundas stated that Standard Vacuum, owned jointly by Socony Vacuum and Standard Oil of New Jersey, did a considerable amount of business in Ethiopia and had long considered an oil concession there. The Company, therefore, had negotiated earlier in the year with Rickett, who was reputed to have experience in securing such concessions. It had organized the African Exploration and Development Corporation for the specific purpose of operating the concession. The two officers insisted that their company had handled the matter in the regular course of business as a private transaction with Ethiopia, and that neither other governments nor officials of the parent organization knew of it. Because of the misleading news coverage and the political complications, they considered it necessary to give the State Department the facts.[25]

After this revelation a meeting between the two oil executives and Hull was arranged for later in the afternoon. The Secretary thought that only an immediate and unconditional withdrawal from the concession would relieve the United States of its embarrassment and ease the tense situation. Walden, taken aback at Hull's strongly worded advice, stated that the present situation and the cancellation of a lease were unparalleled in Standard Oil history. The Company, however, agreed to do as the State Department proposed.[26]

Rumors that the State Department had brought pressure to bear on the American company to cancel the concession greatly disturbed Haile Selassie. He summoned Chargé Engert on September 4 and asked if these rumors were true. The Emperor said he would regret the cancellation very much. He added that he had intended the concession as a sign of his friendliness toward America and his appreciation for the sympathetic interest Americans were showing toward Ethiopia.[27]

Roosevelt and Hull were relieved by the peaceable ending of the Rickett affair. The United States was not yet involved in the controversy, and the two leaders had no desire to complicate the issue or to make it any more difficult for Britain to arrange a solution by negotiation. Hull hoped Engert would convince the Emperor that the State Department had intervened solely to strengthen the hand of the peace-loving powers, including the United States.[28] Roosevelt remarked that the termination of the concession had cleared the air for conferences and negotiations at Geneva. He added, "This is another proof that since March 4, 1933, dollar diplomacy is no longer recognized by the American Government."[29]

Undoubtedly, Haile Selassie had granted the concession in the hope that the United States government would act to protect an American concessionaire and in so doing would be obliged to protect Ethiopia as well. The Emperor had attempted a similar maneuver earlier in the year when he had sought unsuccessfully to reach an agreement with Great Britain on a dam at Lake Tana.[30] But Haile Selassie's diplomacy belonged to the nineteenth century. He could not possibly comprehend such diverse and complicated feelings as American isolationism or the idealism which lay at the heart of the American sympathy for him and his country.

The American public, as their opinions were recorded during 1935 in letters to the editor, newspaper articles and editorials, resolutions of various private organizations, and communications to the President and the Secretary of State, sympathized overwhelmingly with Ethiopia. Most Americans deplored the thought of aggression in Ethiopia or anywhere else, and enthusiastically approved the moral exhortations Roosevelt and Hull had read to Fascist Italy. These sentiments were especially prominent in peace societies, church groups, women's clubs, and labor organizations.

On July 17, 1935, the National Peace Conference, an organization representing 28 nationwide peace, religious, civic, and women's groups, reached agreement on a resolution that the United States should consult with the League of Nations and Kellogg-Briand Pact signatories to assist in finding a peaceful and just solution of the dispute. But the Conference was hopelessly divided on what consultation involved, as well as on what effective measures would aid Ethiopia and preserve peace. Only a small faction, led by the League of Nations Association and supported editorially by the *New York Times,* favored a promise that the United States would not interfere with whatever collective action other states undertook. This faction also endorsed the State Department's proposal for a flexible embargo by which the United States might discriminate against an aggressor.[31]

Protestant groups, through the Federal Council of Churches and their own denominational organizations, played a particularly active part in the peace movement, arousing public sympathy for Ethiopia as the world's oldest Christian nation. During August 1935 special prayers were offered for Ethiopia in most Protestant churches. The *Christian Century,* a leading independent Protestant journal, declared on August 7, "We cannot be interested in general world peace without being interested in specific episodes which threaten to destroy it." But the same issue severely criticized the administration's failure to support the mandatory neutrality legislation introduced by Senators Nye and Clark. In the face of the impending "attack by the fascist dictator on an inoffensive people," the *Christian Century* insisted on "the right to stay neutral at whatever cost."[32]

One factor in the Protestant support for Ethiopia was the fear of what might happen to the thriving Protestant missionary activities there if Catholic Italy occupied the country. As a high missionary official wrote to the State Department, "The experience we have already had in Eritrea where the Swedish mission has experienced exceeding great difficulties in maintaining their work is an indication of what we may have to fear in connection with any extension of Italy's power."[33] (Conversely, some American Catholics approved of Italian occupation because of the encouragement it would give Catholicism.)

American Jews sympathized with Ethiopia as being, like Germany's Jews, a victim of Fascist aggression. In a September 20 editorial, the *American Hebrew and Jewish Tribune* criticized *Time* for describing Haile Selassie as "the acquisitive, Semitic Emperor," and remarked that "the acquisitive bent seems to us to be more evident in Mussolini's hankering for a chunk of Ethiopia or the subjection of that kingdom." The *Jewish Frontier*, organ of the League for Labor Palestine, warned that minority peoples and mandated countries might share the fate of Ethiopia and should therefore watch the Italo-Ethiopian situation with their own interests very much in mind.[34]

American Catholics were less united in sympathy for Ethiopia than Protestants and Jews. Whereas Catholics readily agreed on denouncing the "bolshevistic fanatics" and "hypocritical gangsters" that governed anti-clerical Mexico, they were equivocal toward the Italo-Ethiopian conflict. The large number of Italian-American Catholics and the difficult position of the Pope, himself an Italian, strongly affected Catholic opinion.[35]

At least one Catholic paper, however, the weekly *Pilot* of the Archdiocese of Boston, showed the same concern for peace and international morality that animated other religious groups. Without mentioning Italy or Mussolini by name, the *Pilot* warned of the "fearful responsibility a man assumes who cold-bloodedly precipitates a war." In another column, it was more explicit: "Italy wants to expand; she wishes a colony where her interests may be developed. The alleged affront to Italian dignity is little more than a pretext for attacking Ethiopia." The anti-Italian attitude of the Irish-Catholic *Pilot* undoubtedly reflected religious and political rivalries between Irish and Italian Catholics.[36]

Both the *Commonweal,* an independent, liberal Catholic weekly, and *America,* a Jesuit review, were more cautious than the *Pilot* and had greater sympathy for Italy. Their attitude was ambivalent, however, showing concern for international law and peace machinery but refusing to judge the disputants. Both journals characterized British policy as self-interested, complained that the

League of Nations was dominated by selfish states, and criticized Great Britain and France for not rewarding Italy with colonial compensations after the First World War. *America,* following the lead of the Pope, concluded that no matter how badly Italy had fared in the past, two wrongs did not make a right. "But if war comes to Europe, we know that its origin is no war for the liberation of mankind, but a fight over the division of ill-gotten goods." The United States should therefore not become involved.[37]

American Negroes also took a great interest in the Italo-Ethiopian dispute, especially at this early stage. *Crisis,* the official organ of the National Association for the Advancement of Colored People, saw the conflict as "a sad spectacle of 'white' civilization." *Opportunity,* the journal of the National Urban League, suggested that the Anglo-French efforts to prevent war were motivated not by a genuine regard for Ethiopia's rights but by fear of the effect of a war on their own colonies and the threat of a worldwide challenge to white supremacy.[38] (Both Negro magazines featured articles and editorials in almost every issue during 1935.) Few Negroes realized that the racially proud Amharas who ruled Ethiopia considered themselves Caucasians, and in recent times had themselves held Negro slaves.

Racial extremists and political opportunists excited Negroes into boycotting Italian peddlers and smashing the windows of Italian shopkeepers. Communists dramatized the Italo-Ethiopian crisis in an effort to rally aroused Negroes into Communist-front organizations such as the American League Against War and Fascism. Riots continually erupted between Negroes and Italian-Americans in adjacent neighborhoods. In Jersey City, Negroes taunted Italians over Joe Louis's knockout of the Italian boxer Primo Carnera. Italians responded by boasting about what Mussolini would do to Ethiopia. (The response of Italian-Americans at the height of their activity and influence will be considered in Chapter Nine.) Some Negroes like Herbert Julian, the "Black Eagle of Harlem," and John C. Robinson, the "Brown Condor of Ethiopia," volunteered for service in Ethiopia. Their activities in East Africa, however, contributed more to American newspaper stories than to Ethiopian defense.[39]

The great anxiety aroused in the peace movement by the Italo-Ethiopian crisis led to the establishment in mid-August of an in-

terdenominational and interracial committee to unify and direct
American sympathy for Ethiopia. The American Committee on
the Ethiopian Crisis announced its intention to oppose Italy's
deliberate violation of international ethics, to aid Ethiopia by
peaceful means to preserve its political and territorial sovereignty,
and, in the event of war, to send medical and nonmilitary aid to
the Christian kingdom. The Committee drew support particularly
from the League of Nations Association, the Federal Council of
Churches, and the Ethiopian Consul in New York, John Shaw.[40]
But because of factional differences and the lack of strong popular
support, the Committee had only limited success.

Although the Italo-Ethiopian dispute interested most Americans
and their sympathies were mostly with the underdog Ethiopia,
their concern rarely led them so far as to support effective action.
The fear of involving the United States in international obligations and wars was still uppermost in American minds.

Chapter Four

The United States and Italy

For more than a decade after the First World War, Italy and the United States were on excellent terms. American Ambassador to Italy Richard Washburn Child had assisted Mussolini with an autobiography and had written a laudatory foreword to it. Former Secretary of State Henry L. Stimson, who in October 1935 urged cooperation with the League of Nations against Italian aggression, had earlier considered Fascist Italy the "least difficult" of the European powers and Mussolini "a sound and useful leader."[1]

The change in administration in March 1933 did not alter the good relations between the two countries. President Roosevelt commented in a personal letter that he was "keeping in fairly close touch with the admirable gentleman," as he described Mussolini.[2] Mussolini demonstrated considerable interest in the New Deal experiment, professing to see a similarity between it and Fascism. But the Fascist program of aggressive expansion in 1935 signaled the turning point in Italian-American relations.[3]

In making his plans for the conquest of Ethiopia, Mussolini ignored the United States. Great Britain and France were of far greater importance. Only if one or both of them led the League of Nations in opposition to Italy would the attitude of the United States become important. Italian Ambassador Rosso's telegram of June 25, 1935, confirmed Mussolini's expectations of a disinterested American policy. Rosso referred to statements by Prime Minister Stanley Baldwin and Anthony Eden, Minister for League of Nations Affairs, urging closer relations between Great Britain and the United States. He assured Mussolini, however, that the State Department had not responded with "great enthusiasm to the British advances." (In the early summer of 1935 it was still possible for an Italian diplomat to analyze the American position with reasonable objectivity and at the same time please Mussolini.)[4] Rosso attributed this noncommittal attitude to the President's "preoccupation with internal political questions," to a public and Congressional sentiment "decisively hostile" to United States involvement in European affairs, and to the State Department's "sense of distrust and suspicion" because of Britain's "equivocal policy" during the Manchurian crisis.

While the Italian Ambassador assured Mussolini that the United States would not take "an interest in the complicated European situation," the government-controlled Italian press converted this disinterest into approval. Receiving precise daily directives from the Ministry of Popular Culture and sometimes from Mussolini himself, Italian journalists portrayed Italy, its ambitions, and its friends in the most favorable light.[5] Italian newspapers consistently conveyed the impression to their readers that Italian-Americans remained patriots of the mother country, and that most Americans recognized the just rights and needs of Italy in East Africa.[6]

In a crude but not atypical article, the New York correspondent of *Il Corriere della Sera* interpreted American opinion for his Milanese readers. Because of America's large Negro population and its years of experience with "the primitive psychology of the colored races," he said, America, more than other countries in the world, could appreciate the reasons for Italy's policy in Ethiopia. He even suggested that Ethiopian admission to the League of Nations in 1923 corresponded to the emancipation of the American Negro following the Civil War: if 70 years of freedom in civilized America had not altered the "semi-barbarism" and "incurable immaturity" of American Negroes, how could one expect that a mere decade of membership in the League of Nations would do so for Ethiopia? The correspondent concluded that "America knows the Negro well and understands how to treat him" by keeping him in his place. "Now many Americans are curious to know if, as would be logical, one could institute a Jim Crow diplomatic car on the international train which leads to Geneva."[7]

While the Italian press was claiming American sympathy, the United States was carefully following the developing crisis during 1935. When Rosso described the mobilization of troops and the dispatch of reinforcements to Somaliland and Eritrea as mere precautionary measures, Chief of Near Eastern Affairs Murray reported that according to American sources in Rome, factories were working full shifts producing war materials, and men and supplies were being transported secretly by night; in short, Italy intended an extensive campaign in Ethiopia. Hull thought Rosso had "stretched our credulity beyond the point of elasticity."[8]

Several times during the spring Italian diplomats in Washington and Rome asked the United States government to halt shipments of cars and military supplies to Ethiopia. The Italians complained that such shipments strengthened Ethiopia's intransigent tendencies and made a peaceful resolution of the dispute more difficult. The American government, however, had no authority to restrict such private trade even if it wanted to. Murray said that the Italians had "lost all sense of proportion"; such a restriction by the United States, he thought, would cause a storm of protest in America.[9]

During the summer of 1935 Italian apprehensions were aroused by Hull's reminders of the obligations of the Kellogg-Briand Pact and the State Department's efforts to cooperate with British compromise plans. If the United States went no further than moral exhortation, Italy would be annoyed but not checked. But there was always the possibility that Great Britain and the United States might take concerted action to prevent the planned invasion.

Hull's original, vague reply to Haile Selassie's request for application of the Kellogg-Briand Pact encouraged Italian officials, who contrasted the helpful attitude of the United States with the intransigence of Great Britain.[10] The Italian press claimed that the United States had avoided any pledge to the Pact and that the American government would refuse to interfere in the Italo-Ethiopian dispute. The press contended that the reply to Haile Selassie's appeal was immediate because a delay would have permitted vari-

ous "pseudo-religious and pseudo-political Americans" to flood
Washington with petitions in favor of intervention. Such reason-
ing admittedly hinted at the existence of anti-Italian sentiment in
America, but newspapers assured their readers that agitation in
favor of intervention would only produce an immediate counter-
reaction from Italian-Americans. Furthermore, they claimed that
American authorities "realized the futility of obstructing the necessary Italian operation in East Africa."[11]

The manner in which the Fascist press sought to demonstrate
American acquiescence in Italian ambitions had forced Hull into
a less equivocal position on July 12. The Secretary's second statement eventually appeared in Italian papers, but it received little
or no editorial comment; La Tribuna stated merely that Rosso and
Hull had held a "cordial conversation." Chargé Alexander Kirk in
Rome, who had commented earlier on "the habitual tendency of
newspapers here to glean evidences of support from all possible
sources," reported that the local press had received instructions not
to discuss the subject. Hull's second statement did not constitute
appropriate evidence.[12]

Haile Selassie's appeal and the two American responses received
worldwide publicity, which forced Italy to ponder its relations with
the rest of the world, especially the United States, and to consider
its obligations as a signatory of the Kellogg-Briand Pact. Declarations about settling international disputes by peaceful means irked
Italians, who now feared that American neutrality might not be
enough to prevent world disapproval of Italy's aggressive plan or
to preclude indirect support of measures designed to punish Italy.
In an article probably by Mussolini himself, Il Popolo d'Italia
noted sarcastically that "our worst opposition comes not from the
Harlem Negroes . . . but from many genuine white men in Europe and America."[13]

In editorials on August 3 the Italian press claimed that "Italy
seeks only neutrality" from other countries. British neutrality,
they explained, "supposes the refusal to furnish Ethiopians with
military means and equipment, the supply of which at the present
moment can only lead to an increase in Ethiopian aggressiveness
against Italy." United States neutrality would suppose, in addition, "abstention from any movement which, under the mask of
the most humanitarian and internationalist propositions, results

only in encouraging Ethiopian intransigence and aggression and thus in increasing the impossibility of reaching a peaceful solution which will satisfy the recognized needs of Italy."[14]

The editorials referred to a recent German promise to refrain from supplying arms to Ethiopia as "one of these proofs of neutrality and correctness which Italy appreciates and suggests as an example to other countries." They concluded ominously that the attitude of other states might "create the premise for a future revision of the European balance of power." Not only did Italy warn the United States to remain strictly neutral, it also delivered a thinly veiled threat to Great Britain and France that Italy might join hands with Germany.

Referring to the Kellogg-Briand Pact, *Giornale* Editor Virginio Gayda insisted that "no pact and not even membership in the League of Nations can give Ethiopia impunity [to defy Italy]. No treaty and no article of the Covenant can deprive Italy of the right of legitimate defense, of security, and of the protection of her honor." Italian journalists, diplomats, and propagandists brusquely dismissed the relevance of the Kellogg-Briand Pact, arguing that Italy had excluded specific geographical areas just as Great Britain had. More important, however, the Italians pointed out that the Pact permitted military action in self-defense.[15] Since modern states do not admit going to war except in such cases, Italy could easily evade the obligations of the international agreement.

Despite its increasing vexation, the Italian press remained unwilling to antagonize the United States or to sacrifice the pretense that Americans sympathized with Italy. Kirk noted in early August that the Italian press had violently attacked several countries, especially Great Britain, while giving others like France and Germany favorable treatment. "As an example of a middle course," Kirk concluded, "may be cited the case of the United States where a contentious attitude on the part of the Italian newspapers has been clearly absent."[16]

Several times during the summer the State Deparment advised the British government of American policies. For example, it informed the Foreign Office in advance of the President's proposed August 1 press statement—planned to coincide with an important session of the League Council—which would reiterate the American hope for a peaceful solution of the Italo-Ethiopian dispute. Chargé Atherton in London asked Foreign Secretary Hoare if he knew of "some element in the situation of which we are not aware and which makes it desirable to delay."[17] The United States desired to cooperate with British efforts for a reasonable compromise solution.

In Washington on August 12, British Ambassador Ronald Lindsay suggested to Under Secretary William Phillips that a real crisis was approaching in compromise negotiations among Great Britain, France, and Italy. He wondered if the American government might again speak out in favor of a peaceful solution of the dispute. The British considered the United States a great moral force, and Lindsay thought an American message at the right moment might have a salutary effect.

Three days later the State Department instructed the embassies in London and Paris to keep it closely informed of all developments at the approaching Paris meeting of the three powers. It asked "the benefit of all information which would enable the American Government to determine whether any further action by it within the limits of its established policy and its obligations as a signatory to the Pact of Paris would be likely to have a beneficial rather than disadvantageous effect." Hull wanted to be sure that any further action by the American government would "contribute toward the effort being put forth by the British and other governments similarly interested in the preservation of peace."[18]

Chargé Theodore J. Marriner in Paris responded on August 17 with a report of a long discussion with Alexis Léger, the Permanent Secretary General of the Quai d'Orsay. Léger believed that Mussolini understood neither the seriousness of the situation nor the true sentiments of other nations because Italian ambassadors did not dare to report the truth. He suggested that Mussolini was hoping the United States would remain at least disinterested. It might serve a useful purpose, he concluded, if the President or the Secretary of State would suggest to the Italian Ambassador that the United States would regard failure to achieve a peaceful solution of the dispute as a world calamity. To make certain that Mussolini received the full content of this message, Léger advised sending a second copy to the American Embassy in Rome. Later the same day, Anthony Eden and Robert Vansittart, who was Permanent Under Secretary for Foreign Affairs, agreed with Léger that the United States might profitably support the Anglo-French compromise effort by making a direct appeal to Mussolini.[19]

As soon as he received these telegrams from Paris, Hull conferred with Roosevelt, who suggested writing a personal note, as President, to the Italian Prime Minister. On August 18 Hull instructed Kirk to seek an immediate interview with Mussolini to deliver the President's message. In the note Roosevelt expressed his "earnest hope that the controversy between Italy and Ethiopia will be resolved without recourse to armed conflict." He warned Mussolini that "failure to arrive at a peaceful settlement of the present dispute and a subsequent outbreak of hostilities would be a world calamity the consequences of which would adversely affect the interests of all nations."[20] Kirk had delivered the note on August 19, in a personal interview with Mussolini, but the Paris negotiations had already collapsed because of the Italian demand for a large-scale cession of Ethiopian territory and a mandate over the remainder.

Mussolini had not misunderstood the purpose of the President's personal message, but it was actions, not words, that influenced him. In his conversation with Kirk, Mussolini was confident and courteous, but blunt when he explained that Italian mobilization and expenditures made it too late to avoid an armed conflict and that the United States could not expect Italy to draw back and thus sacrifice its prestige. British support, Mussolini continued, had enabled Haile Selassie to strengthen his position enough so that Italy could secure its legitimate interests only by military victory. Since Italy required the occupation of Ethiopia, Britain should have known that the Anglo-French proposals at Paris would be unacceptable. Italy, he concluded, intended to carry out its military action regardless of the League of Nations. If opposition by other countries developed into actual interference, such as closing the Suez Canal to Italian use, Italy would regard such measures as hostile and react accordingly.[21]

When Roosevelt received Kirk's report of this encounter with Mussolini, he told Hull "it is never too late to avoid an armed conflict"; it would enhance rather than harm Italian prestige, he said, if "Italy could take the magnificent position that rather than

resort to war she would cancel the military preparations and submit the whole question to peaceful settlement by arbitration."[22]

Neither Italy nor the United States released Roosevelt's message to Mussolini to the press. Kirk had urged that the State Department keep the message secret in order not to antagonize the
Italians unnecessarily or to give them an opportunity to twist the
message to their own purposes.[23] Italian newspapers, however,
could no longer ignore the public and private American appeals
for a peaceful settlement. They now stated that the United States
might join Britain in "platonic manifestations against the war"
but that it would never involve itself in an actual conflict. They
assured their readers, moreover, that Americans were beginning
to suspect the apparent British zeal in support of the League and
to question British disinterest.[24]

The approval by Congress and the President of a neutrality resolution without the discretionary embargo came as a relief to Italy.
In the event of war, this meant that the United States could not
single out Italy for more than moral condemnation, since the embargo on arms, ammunition, and implements of war applied to
Ethiopia as well. This fact might discourage the League from taking effective action, and in addition the door would remain open
for Italian trade with America even if the League did invoke sanctions. The Italians, therefore, considered the temporary victory
of the Congressional isolationists as a respite for themselves. In
a press interview, Mussolini approved the American action by
advising Great Britain to "follow the example of the United States
and leave us alone to fulfill our mission."[25]

The announcement, on August 31, of Haile Selassie's desperate
effort to draw the United States to Ethiopia's support by granting
an extensive mineral concession to an American firm astonished
the Italians. Ambassador Long commented that one Foreign Office
official had no idea of the background of the concession and did
not even want to discuss the matter. Italy virtually ignored the
part played by Americans in the concession, and the press carefully avoided antagonizing the United States. Italian journalists
occasionally referred to the concessionaire as "Anglo-American,"
but argued that it was "probably English in substance and American only in form." They blasted the British bitterly, alleging hy-

pocrisy in preaching moral platitudes while effecting an imperialist scheme that used the United States as a shield.[26]

With the news from Washington that the Standard Vacuum
Company had admitted full responsibility for the concession and
had canceled it at the insistence of the State Department, the Italian press abruptly dropped the story. Ambassador Long reported
that Hull's statements and the oil company's renunciation had
made a very favorable impression on Italians, who considered the
outcome of the incident substantial proof of American neutrality.[27]

Active American intervention on behalf of Ethiopia did not
worry Italy; the cancellation of the concession had clearly indicated the improbability of that. Italians feared, however, that the
United States government, despite the neutrality resolution and
the nondiscriminatory embargo, might encourage action by the
League of Nations and somehow cooperate with it. Roosevelt
and Hull had demonstrated their sentiments during the past few
months in the several appeals for a peaceful solution, the support
of Anglo-French negotiations, and the campaign for a discretionary embargo.

Mussolini's son-in-law Galeazzo Ciano, the Minister of Popular
Culture, commented privately that American "public opinion is
dead against us in the Abyssinian question."[28] In September 1935,
therefore, Ciano sent Commendatore Bernardo Bergamaschi on
a special mission to the United States "to study the possibilities
for our propaganda in the present political crisis."[29]

The Italian government was contemplating a publicity effort
to counteract what it considered the highly effective and insidious
propaganda of the British. Unable to understand how anyone
could regard their country as guilty of a serious breach of international morality, or to comprehend how anyone not personally
or selfishly interested could sympathize with the Ethiopians, Italians looked for a malign influence and found it in British propaganda. American revisionist historians gave credence to the Italian
case in their contention that skillful Allied propaganda had helped
to drag the United States into war in 1917.[30]

The report that Bergamaschi submitted to Ciano on October
18, 1935, reflected conditions in the United States quite accurately,
except for an overemphasis on British pressure and propaganda.
It outlined frankly and succinctly the vagaries of American public

opinion, the relation of the United States to the Italo-Ethiopian dispute, and the attitude of the administration and Congress. It was not, Bergamaschi pointed out, "a comforting picture." Governing circles, especially the White House and the State Department, tended to heed British advice and as a result lacked sympathy for Italy. They pretended to be neutral but actually favored Britain and the League. Only because of Senate action in the recent neutrality debate did "the *isolationist* tendency" triumph over "*collaborationism* with regard to the Italo-Ethiopian conflict."[31] Other than Italian-Americans, and to some extent the Catholic Church, Bergamaschi counted few Italian sympathizers in the United States. Nevertheless, he realized that the determination of isolationists to avoid foreign complications might constitute a vital lever in preventing actions harmful to Italy. Their successful effort to block the administration's desire for a discretionary embargo had illustrated the important role they played.

Bergamaschi enclosed in his report a prospectus by a New York public relations firm for a publicity campaign to combat the unfavorable American reaction to Italian ambitions in Ethiopia. It suggested offsetting the adverse effect of military headlines from Ethiopia by news of great cultural and humanitarian benefits accomplished by Italy in Tripoli and Rhodes. "It will be a natural inference that countless benefits will likewise result from the occupation of Ethiopia by Italy." The company also recommended that judicious advertising in selected American newspapers would secure untold benefits in the papers' benevolent treatment of Italian affairs. After all, the prospectus concluded, American businesses do it all the time!

Bergamaschi denied the notion that Americans stubbornly opposed all forms of propaganda. Indeed, he considered Americans more susceptible to propaganda than any other people. Since Great Britain was pursuing the same methods that had led the United States to intervention in 1917, Bergamaschi concluded that "the greatest care in the preparation and timely execution of an adequate counter-propaganda is more than ever before necessary on our part." Italy considered it vital that the United States and Great Britain not cooperate in any activities that might hinder Italian ambitions in East Africa.

Chapter Five

The American Neutrality Resolution

The Joint Resolution on Neutrality of August 1935 was the result of a compromise between the administration and its isolationist foes in Congress. The administration had sought a discretionary embargo on arms, ammunition, and implements of war in order to retain control over foreign policy and to cooperate with other nations in preserving the peace. Isolationists in Congress, however, had feared that a flexible policy by an internationalist President might involve the United States in foreign entanglements and ultimately force the country into war. With the Italo-Ethiopian conflict approaching and the neutrality bloc threatening to filibuster, Congress and the President compromised on a six-month embargo applicable to both belligerents.

The resolution empowered the President to define the terms "arms, ammunition, and implements of war," and it gave him the responsibility of determining when a state of war existed and whether the arms embargo should apply at the outbreak of hostilities or during their progress. At his discretion the President could extend the embargo to other states if the war spread to them and forbid Americans to travel on vessels of belligerent powers except at their own risk.

President Roosevelt pointed out privately that the neutrality legislation "takes away little Executive authority except the embargo on certain types of arms and munitions (the type to be determined by me) between now and next February."[1] But what use would the administration make of its discretionary power? Would it extend the definition of arms, ammunition, and implements of war to include vital raw materials, such as oil, cotton, and copper? The action that the League of Nations might take against an aggressor could depend on the attitude of the United States toward restricting trade with the aggressor, especially in the case of these important raw materials. During early September the State Department considered what articles to enumerate in the embargo. For the sake of efficient administration, Hull recommended the inclusion of only actual military armaments and supplies.[2] On September 25 the President proclaimed the list, as the neutrality resolution required him to do.

This decision to give a narrow definition to arms, ammunition, and implements of war, however, was made reluctantly and may have been only provisional. After a cabinet meeting on September 24 in which members had discussed the Italo-Ethiopian situation, Secretary of the Interior Harold L. Ickes concluded that Hull intended "to classify, and then prohibit the export thereof as articles of war, certain raw materials the withholding of which would seriously impair the ability of Italy to fight to a successful conclusion." In several off-the-record comments, State Department officials emphasized that the administration could extend the list if it chose. Secretary of Commerce Daniel C. Roper repeated that the government was still considering other commodities that "could be added in light of future developments."[3]

During September State Department officials also considered other phases of the neutrality resolution in the context of the approaching Italo-Ethiopian War. The Division Chiefs of Near Eastern and Western European Affairs, Wallace Murray and Joseph C. Green, agreed that Congress had intended that the President proclaim the arms embargo as soon as any hostilities began, with or without a declaration of war. Murray suggested, however, that if Italy should initiate hostilities against Great Britain or other members of the League for trying to impose sanctions, the President had sufficient authority to refrain indefinitely from extending the arms embargo to these countries. Congress may not have intended to grant this discretion, Murray admitted, but he felt that public opinion would warmly support such a stand pending the reconvening of Congress in January. Keeping in mind that the President did not legally have to take action immediately upon the outbreak of hostilities, but instead could do so during the progress of the war, Murray wondered if the President might not appropriately and safely synchronize his action with whatever program the League of Nations might follow. "In that way," he said, "a solution might be found to the question of whether Italy is engaged in war or hostilities with Ethiopia, and we should have the advantage of working in unison with the League members rather than on our own in bringing pressure upon Italy."[4]

Hull feared that hostilities between Italy and Ethiopia might break out during Roosevelt's fishing cruise in October. On September 25, presuming that the President would want to proclaim the neutrality embargo without delay, Hull prepared a draft proclamation for Roosevelt, who signed and returned it. Hull promised to keep in close contact with the President on his cruise, especially if the occasion for issuance of the proclamation arose.[5]

One can ascertain without difficulty, throughout the Italo-Ethiopian crisis, what the State Department learned from its representatives abroad and what response it made. It is not so easy, however, to determine how the American government decided on a particular policy or why it took a specific action. Roosevelt preferred personal conversations to staff conferences or written reports. Moreover, his subordinates often found his thinking enigmatic, and their memoirs offer few clues to the rationale of the administration's policies, especially its foreign policy.[6]

In early October, however, with Roosevelt on his fishing cruise, Hull transmitted government business via telegraph as he had promised. The large number of these telegrams exchanged from October 3 to October 5 have preserved the viewpoints and arguments of the President and his Secretary of State.[7] A long personal letter from Joseph C. Green, who participated in the State Department discussions of the embargo proclamation, to the American Minister in Switzerland, Hugh R. Wilson, described the opinions of high State Department officials and the way they reached their final decision.[8]

On October 3, 1935, Italy informed the world that Ethiopia had finally succeeded in starting a war.[9] Italian planes bombed Adowa and Adigrat as had been planned months before. The Council of the League of Nations met immediately to determine what action, if any, it should take in the face of these hostilities.

Roosevelt, aboard the *U.S.S. Houston* in the Pacific, instructed Hull to issue the previously signed proclamation if he had official confirmation of the Italian invasion and of battles and casualties well within the Ethiopian border. Roosevelt thought that hostilities of this nature would constitute war within the meaning of the neutrality resolution. He suggested publicizing the names of American citizens sailing on Italian ships and the cargo manifests of all vessels shipping goods to either belligerent. He also proposed that the Secretary of the Treasury check credit extensions by American banks to either side.[10]

On the *Houston* Secretary Ickes reported great interest in the Italo-Ethiopian situation; "the sympathies of everyone were with Ethiopia," he said. According to Harry Hopkins, Roosevelt "scanned the news dispatches and everything favorable to Ethiopia brought a loud 'Good.' "[11] But the President did not take kindly the suggestion that he should cut short his cruise and return to Washington because of the crisis. Roosevelt himself prepared a news release saying that he was "receiving almost hourly bulletins from Washington covering the foreign situation." In fact, the release went on, "the complete freedom from a constant stream of callers and telephone messages" was enabling the President to relax for the first time in six months and "to give quiet consideration to the nation's foreign and domestic policies."[12]

Meanwhile, Hull in Washington had telegraphed the American representatives in London, Paris, Rome, Geneva, and Addis Ababa, asking whether this was merely another border incursion or the long-expected invasion. Since neither side had issued a declaration of war, he wanted to know if hostilities actually had broken out and if, in fact, war was in progress.[13]

Ambassador Long replied quickly from Rome with the text of the official Italian communiqué admitting penetration of Ethiopian territory and quoting General de Bono's invasion proclamation to the Ethiopians. He also forwarded Italian newspaper reports of the heroism of Ciano and of Mussolini's two young sons on the first day of hostilities. Long urged that in order to avoid the presumption of American collaboration with the League of

Nations, the State Department issue the neutrality proclamation before the League could take action. Ambassador Bingham from London answered on October 4 that the British government did not recognize a state of war because of the absence of an official declaration, but that British officials anticipated action by the League that would presumably alter the legal situation.[14]

From Thursday night, October 3, to late Saturday, October 5, high State Department officials gathered in Hull's office in almost continuous session. They discussed the question of when they should issue the embargo proclamation and what kind of statement the President should make to accompany it. On the timing of the embargo proclamation, three viewpoints emerged, though everyone agreed that American action had to precede the League decision in order to maintain the carefully cultivated fiction of American independence. One opinion, backed by Assistant Secretary Moore and Arms Control Chief Green, and in part by Secretary Hull, urged the immediate issuance of the proclamation in order to avoid without question the appearance of cooperation with the League of Nations. Under Secretary Phillips and Near Eastern and Far Eastern Division Chiefs Murray and Hornbeck favored delaying the proclamation as long as possible, at least until the League had indicated the direction of its decision. Legal Adviser Hackworth, Economic Adviser Feis, and Western European Affairs Division Chief Dunn advocated delaying even longer, until just before the League decision went into effect. The latter two viewpoints counseled a wait-and-see attitude so as not to prejudice League action in any way.[15]

Because of this indecision on the timing of the embargo proclamation, Hull telegraphed Minister Wilson in Switzerland on Friday afternoon, asking specifically about the probability of League action the next day. Hull then replied to Roosevelt's earlier communication, which had authorized him to issue the neutrality proclamation as soon as he had confirmed the Italian invasion. Hull now advised delaying at least until the next morning, when he expected to hear from Wilson and also to receive further, more official proof of war.[16]

Wilson telephoned Hull from Geneva just before noon on Saturday, October 5, saying that he thought the League Council would reach no decision before Monday afternoon, and strongly urging that the United States not take the first step in recognizing hostilities. Wilson argued that the League would find it difficult to achieve unanimity on the question. He particularly feared that if the United States proclaimed its neutrality before the League declared a violation of the Covenant, some League members might use the American embargo proclamation as an excuse to declare their own neutrality and thus frustrate collective action by the League.

Hull admitted in his telephone conversation with Wilson that the government had some flexibility in the timing of the embargo proclamation, but that the American public would expect action without unreasonable delay: "You probably understand we want to state our attitude about trade with the belligerent countries before a formal request is made of us about sanctions. . . . That means a great deal over here and that is our motive in being rather prompt to proclaim this embargo." Wilson repeatedly assured Hull that the United States would have plenty of time to take action under the neutrality resolution after the League had made a decision but before the Council had discussed its implementation.[17]

Hull, who earlier had favored immediate proclamation of the arms embargo, found Wilson's arguments impressive, especially the one that an immediate proclamation might discourage collective action by the League. Hull immediately telegraphed Roosevelt, advising him that he now had sufficient evidence to warrant issuing the proclamation and that the Department had everything in readiness to do so, but that he, nevertheless, favored a delay until Monday. Since the Council presumably would reach a decision on Monday, a delay until just prior to the Council session would have the advantage of demonstrating the independence of American policy without unduly prejudicing League action.

Hull was far more cautious than Roosevelt on the questions of publicizing cargo manifests and the names of merchants and passengers using Italian ships, and he recommended that these rather drastic actions be held in reserve. In the event of developments that might jeopardize American neutrality, he suggested that the President might first issue an appeal and then a threat to make public these names and facts.[18]

While telegraphers were transmitting Hull's long message on Saturday afternoon, a telegram arrived from Roosevelt approving Hull's draft to accompany the neutrality proclamation but strongly reiterating the need to issue the additional statement about passenger travel on belligerent ships. The intent of the legislation, the President insisted, "is to prevent aid to either belligerent, and American passenger travel on Italian ships gives aid not only financially but also by making access to Italy more easy for Americans seeking commercial advantages. I strongly urge that the record of strict adherence to spirit of [the] Act be maintained." Hull continued transmitting his long message, adding a cautious objection that Italy might construe such a statement as a "gratuitous affront in the nature of sanctions." Hull concluded that he would await further instructions from Roosevelt.[19]

Almost immediately Hull received another telegram from Roosevelt in response to the first part of the long message. Roosevelt agreed with Ambassador Long that the United States should issue the embargo proclamation before the League took any action, and with Hull that the facts established the existence of actual war. "If you have not already taken action, you are hereby authorized to do so." Hull replied that he was preparing to act that night but was still awaiting comment on the remainder of his long message.[20]

With his patience running out, since he had from the very beginning wanted Hull to issue the proclamation quickly, Roosevelt remarked caustically, "They are dropping bombs on Ethiopia and that is war. Why wait for Mussolini to say so." He wired back 16 minutes later: "It is my judgment that proclamation issue immediately in view of undoubted state of war and without waiting League action."[21]

From noon to midnight on Saturday, October 5, State Department officials still gathered in Hull's office. Moore and Green continued to urge immediate action while the others counseled delay. But when Roosevelt's repeated instructions became categorical, and when Chargé Atherton reported from London late in the afternoon that Foreign Secretary Hoare had no objection whatever to their issuing the proclamation, the State Department could delay the issuance no longer.[22]

The President's telegram demanding that the proclamation be

issued immediately was held up three hours and received by the State Department at 9:50 P.M. At 9:40 P.M. Hull had asked Roosevelt if he had received all of the long afternoon message. While the State Department was acting on the President's categorical demand, Roosevelt replied that he had received all but the third part of Hull's long message. He acquiesced in Hull's insistence that the government hold up for further study the plan for publicizing individual names and cargo manifests.[23]

The State Department issued the arms embargo proclamation at 10:23 P.M., but Hull delayed the proclamation concerning passenger travel on Italian ships pending Roosevelt's reply to the third part of his long message. The President responded immediately that it seemed to him, even if not to Hull, that "Americans sailing on belligerent ships may jeopardize peace or endanger lives or affect commercial interests or security of the United States."[24] Hull then reluctantly issued the additional proclamation.

The administration had thus applied the embargo on the shipment of arms, ammunition, and implements of war to both belligerent countries, as required by the letter of the law and the intent of Congress. The President, in addition, had exercised his discretionary power to warn American citizens that they traveled on belligerent ships at their own risk. Hull had argued, not unreasonably, that Italy might consider this a form of sanctions since Ethiopia had no navy with which to provoke disturbances that might involve Americans. Roosevelt overrode these objections, contending that the spirit of the resolution prohibited aid to belligerents and that the use of Italian vessels constituted aid. At the same time, Roosevelt did not insist on his original suggestion that the government publicize the names of individual passengers and manifests of cargoes on belligerent ships.

The warning included in the statement accompanying the embargo proclamation carried particular significance. "In these specific circumstances," the President declared, "I want it to be understood that any of our people who voluntarily engage in transactions of any character with either of the belligerents do so at their own risk." The administration's interpretation of the spirit of the neutrality resolution marked the beginning of the moral embargo, one of the government's chief tools in seeking to cooperate with the League in applying sanctions against the Italian aggressor.[25]

Minister Wilson in Geneva welcomed the President's clear warning. "The statement is admirable," he said, "in that it proclaims a new policy which I believe creates the best possible defense against the United States being involved in European conflict and is at the same time in harmony with the collective effort to maintain peace."[26]

Chapter Six

The League and Sanctions

Those countries most directly involved in the Italo-Ethiopian crisis had followed with care the development of America's neutrality policy during the late summer of 1935. Italy was encouraged to learn that the arms embargo could not single out one country for American condemnation and that Congress had checked the internationalists who wanted to cooperate with the League of Nations.[1] Haile Selassie, on the other hand, complained of "the lack of justice" in an arms embargo operating equally against aggressor and victim. He agreed, however, that in the present circumstances the American restriction helped the cause of peace, and he expressed hope that when the conflict finally began the United States would support economic measures against Italy.[2]

American neutrality legislation disappointed Great Britain, as it had Ethiopia, because it did not differentiate between aggressor and victim and did not include an embargo on raw materials. Prime Minister Baldwin had stated in November 1934, before the Wal-Wal clash occurred, that he would not act in international affairs until he had ascertained the attitude of the United States. He now knew about the American embargo on arms, ammunition, and implements of war, but he was concerned over what the United States would do about vital raw materials.

Despite its uncertainty over the American attitude, the Council of the League of Nations laid the groundwork during September 1935 for possible action against any aggressor. It met on September 4, as scheduled, for a general consideration of the Italo-Ethiopian dispute. A ridiculous but politic compromise charging neither side with responsibility for the incident had been reached on the previous day and had finally settled the Wal-Wal dispute. Never the real issue anyway, the dispute, and the subsequent negotiations to settle it, had served merely as a façade behind which Mussolini prepared for war against Ethiopia. Now that the invasion was imminent, Wal-Wal could be forgotten.[3]

Mussolini accordingly reversed his strategy and directed Aloisi at Geneva to stop refusing discussion of the Ethiopian situation and to announce and justify Italian plans. At the Council's September 4 meeting, Aloisi presented a long, documented memorandum of Italy's case against Ethiopia, a device suggested by Joseph Avenol, the Italophile Secretary General of the League of Nations.[4] Aloisi's memorandum asserted that Ethiopia had neglected its treaty obligations by blocking boundary delimitations and economic and cultural projects, that it had inflicted many outrages on Italian citizens and diplomats, and that it had demonstrated unfitness for League of Nations membership by tolerating slavery, oppressing minority tribes, and breaking promises. Italian action against Ethiopia would not violate the League Covenant, therefore, but would defend the League's good name in a situation that was intolerable for both the League and Italy. Italy, the document concluded, reserved full liberty to take whatever measures it considered necesssary to protect its interests and safeguard its colonies.[5]

The Italian memorandum included some valid points, but few diplomats in Geneva believed that Mussolini's aims in East Africa were altruistic. Russian Delegate Maxim Litvinov expressed the general view when he asserted that the League could not differentiate between its members on the basis of internal regime or racial stock or degree of civilization. Neither Italy nor any other country could decide on its own that another League state did not merit the rights of League membership.[6]

The Council ignored the Italian rationalizations and on September 7 appointed a committee of five members to study relations between Italy and Ethiopia and seek a peaceful settlement according to Article 15 of the Covenant. This article specified that the Council should provide an opportunity for disputants to reach an agreement, that if they failed to agree the Council should make its own recommendations for a just settlement, and that if one party accepted its recommendations no other party to the dispute could attack it. The Council had thus taken the first of several legal steps that could ultimately lead to a condemnation of an aggressor and the imposition of sanctions against it.

On September 18 the Committee of Five presented its report, which was a plan for international assistance allowing Ethiopian sovereignty and territory to remain largely intact but transferring important administrative functions to experts working under the aegis of the League. The Committee had designed the plan to meet Italian grievances listed in the memorandum of September 4, and Haile Selassie agreed to accept it as a basis for negotiation. Fearing a break with Great Britain, Aloisi in Geneva urged Mussolini to accept the plan, but Ethiopian expert Guariglia in Rome advised against it on the grounds that it guaranteed nothing and might even decrease Italy's influence in Ethiopia. Mussolini rejected the Committee's proposals because they included no endorsement of Italy's claim to a pre-eminent position in Ethiopia.[7]

Enthusiasm for the League and for collective action mounted during September as the British government, pushed increasingly by the pressure of public opinion within Great Britain, appeared to assume leadership. On September 11 Foreign Secretary Hoare electrified the League of Nations Assembly with his declaration that "the League stands, and my country stands with it, for the collective maintenance of the Covenant in its entirety, and particularly for steady and collective resistance to all acts of unprovoked aggression." Hoare insisted that the British determination was "no variable and unreliable sentiment, but a principle of international conduct to which they and their government hold with firm, enduring, and universal persistence."[8] In one of the most dramatic moments of the Italo-Ethiopian crisis, delegation followed delegation in welcoming the apparent British leadership in defense of international law and the rights of small nations.

This contagious enthusiasm spread to Washington, where State Department officials had doubted that the great powers, deeply troubled by the depression and the fear of Germany, would defend Ethiopia against Italian ambitions. As the chorus at Geneva grew, all but the most cynical in Washington saw the League in a new light. Officials who had reached high positions in the government professing the belief that "the League rested on sand," wrote Economic Adviser Feis, "began to wonder whether they were correct."[9]

For some time the State Department had considered another public statement of the American position. Stanley K. Hornbeck, Chief of the Far Eastern Affairs Division, urged on September 11 that the United States take advantage of the meeting of the League Assembly to issue a clear-cut appeal for compliance with the Kellogg-Briand Pact and, in effect, to suggest that the Geneva powers promote such compliance. Hornbeck argued that another reminder of the obligations of the Pact would neither limit American action in the future nor stand in the way of American cooperation with the League of Nations in the event the League asked for it. As the Department's Far Eastern Chief, he undoubtedly hoped that League action against Italy would serve as a pointed warning to Japan, which was continuing to encroach upon China.

Following Hoare's dramatic declaration to the League Assembly that same day, Hornbeck renewed his insistence that the "opportune moment" had come for the American government to indicate its "strong moral support of the effort on behalf of peace which is being made by the British Government and those other of the League powers who stand for that principle."[10]

Consequently, on September 12 Hull issued a long statement reviewing the efforts of the United States during the preceding months to encourage a peaceful settlement of the Italo-Ethiopian dispute. The Secretary's concluding appeal, which had an unmistakably internationalist tone, pointed out that armed "conflict in any part of the world cannot but have undesirable and adverse effects in every part of the world. All nations," he insisted, "have the right to ask that any and all issues, between whatsoever nations, be resolved by pacific means. . . . With good will toward all nations, the American Government asks of those countries which appear to be contemplating armed hostilities that they weigh most solicitously the declaration and pledge given in the Pact of Paris."[11]

In the worldwide enthusiasm aroused by Hoare's opening address to the League Assembly, however, the important qualifications in the address received little attention: "If the burden is to be borne," the British Foreign Secretary had said, "it must be borne collectively. If risks for peace are to be run, they must be run by all. The security of the many cannot be ensured solely by the efforts of the few, however powerful they may be."[12]

Those who applauded Hoare's speech did not know, furthermore, what he had said previously in a private discussion with French Premier Laval. Neither wished to take any action that might disrupt the Stresa front or cause Mussolini to retaliate; from such a split with Italy, they agreed, only Hitler could profit. As Laval later disclosed, "We found ourselves instantaneously in agreement upon ruling out military sanctions, not adopting any measure of a naval blockade, and never contemplating the closure of the Suez Canal—in a word, ruling out everything that might lead to war."[13] The British Undersecretary of State for Foreign Affairs, Viscount Cranborne, made the point more gracefully early in 1936 when he admitted that Laval and Hoare had agreed to limit collective action to "certain economic and financial measures."[14] Hoare may have meant, as his defenders later suggested, to acquiesce in this restriction only for the first round of sanctions. But in any case, there was a discrepancy between his public and his private positions.

The appearance of part of the British Home Fleet at Gibraltar on September 12, the day following Hoare's speech, seemed proof of Great Britain's leadership of the League and the government's determination to punish an aggressor. Yet on September 20, the British Ambassador in Rome assured the Italian government that the presence of British warships in the Mediterranean implied no threat to Italy and had resulted from anti-British attacks in the Italian press. Great Britain thus continued its dual policy. To please world opinion, it defended the Covenant and opposed aggression; at the same time, to avoid taking any positive action, it sought a compromise that would appease Italy.

Meanwhile, American Minister Wilson reported from Geneva that no one had formally raised the question of what the United States would do in the event of League action. In 1933 at the Disarmament Conference, United States Representative Norman Davis had promised that under certain conditions his government would not hinder the efforts of the League to enforce collective security. Recalling this promise, some delegates in Geneva began to show interest in the terms of the American neutrality resolution, especially the question of whether the arms embargo might include raw materials.[15]

Hoare in London and Anthony Eden in Geneva made it clear that they considered the American attitude of the greatest importance. They promised, however, that they would make no requests of the United States now because Great Britain did not wish to act prematurely or to embarrass the United States in any way. Hoare indicated that he would solicit American cooperation after an act of aggression, and Eden reassured Wilson that Britain would consult the United States only after deciding on a definite program and would hope for a "benevolent" American response.[16]

The possibility of a direct public inquiry concerning America's policy particularly worried Hull. Such a question might force the State Department's hand and destroy any chance of cooperation with the League. It pleased Hull, therefore, to learn that Britain did not intend to press the point immediately. Hull explained to Chargé Atherton in London that if Hoare inquired further, he was to be told that the United States "would not join in the imposition of sanctions upon any nation involved in the pending controversy between Italy and Ethiopia." On the question of cooperation with the League, Hull continued, "it would of course be obviously impossible for this Government to arrive at any conclusion with regard thereto before it was placed in full possession of the reasons and basis upon which such collective action by the League were founded and a complete description of the specific measures to be put into effect." He was quite certain, however, "that no advantage could be gained from any premature discussion of hypothetical possibilities in this regard."[17]

Great Britain wished to believe that although the United States had rejected membership in the League of Nations, American sponsorship of the Kellogg-Briand Pact indicated American support for the sanctity of treaties, including the one containing the League Covenant. Hull's statements during the summer showed that the United States had not forgotten the Kellogg-Briand Pact, but they did not reveal whether or not the United States would respond to an appeal for a conference or consultation among the signatories of the Pact.

The State Department was not eager to see the Kellogg-Briand Pact invoked but it would find it difficult to object to a suggestion for mere consultation. Secretary of State Stimson had always said that the Pact included *ipso facto* the idea of consultation, and the Democratic platform of 1932 had advocated consultation in case violation of the Pact was threatened. On the other hand, the purpose of consultation at this time would obviously be for the consideration of sanctions, and this might compel the United States to make a definite decision. If the government agreed to join in collective action, isolationists would be outraged; if it refused, the League of Nations would be greatly discouraged.[18]

Hull tried to dissuade Hoare from any proposal that would invoke the Kellogg-Briand Pact. If such an invocation were to go beyond a mere marshaling of world opinion, Hull argued, the Pact might encroach upon the League of Nations, for it could weaken the Covenant by appearing to be a substitute for it. Moreover, he insisted that the United States had already shown its cooperative attitude, principally by prohibiting loans to the Italian government and restricting credit in trade with Italy. A direct request to the United States for active participation in sanctions or for a conference of Kellogg-Briand Pact signatories could achieve nothing more. Indeed, Hull feared that such action might actually do harm by frightening the American people and thus further tying the hands of those in the Executive branch who wanted to cooperate in the preservation of world peace.[19]

Meanwhile, the talk of sanctions and League action had exasperated Mussolini. He pointed out to Ambassador Long that no one had applied sanctions against the French in Morocco, the Japanese in China, or the British in Iraq or India, or against the Germans for rearming in violation of the Versailles Treaty. But, Mussolini continued bitterly, "when Italy proceeds to rectify wrongs which have been committed against her and to secure the rights of her colonies and to proceed to a legitimate expansion—which even England has recognized—when I proceed, they talk about sanctions!"[20]

Mussolini had not expected his quest for a place in the colonial sun to present such problems. Despite assurances from Laval that Hoare had agreed to limit sanctions,[21] Mussolini was anxious about the possibility of an oil embargo or closure of the Suez Canal as a result of League enthusiasm, British public opinion, and evidence of American willingness to cooperate. When he proclaimed national mobilization on the eve of the October 3 invasion, he declared: "To sanctions of an economic character we will reply with our discipline, with our sobriety, and with our spirit of sacrifice. To sanctions of a military character we will reply with orders of a military character. To acts of war we will reply with acts of war."[22]

The Italian invasion in alleged self-defense was not unexpected, but the immediate action of the Council and the Assembly of the League of Nations surprised Paris and London, and it came as a shock in Rome. On September 26, after Italy had rejected the compromise peace plan of the Committee of Five, the Council had formed itself into the Committee of Thirteen[23] to draft a formal statement and recommendation. Before these could be completed, however, Italy had attacked Ethiopia. The Council met on October 5, two days after the invasion, and reviewed the report of the Committee of Thirteen, which had concluded that neither Italy nor Ethiopia could legitimately resort to arms. In view of the Italian invasion, the Council appointed a committee of six members to study the crisis; it reported on October 7 that Italy had resorted to war in disregard of Article 12 of the League of Nations Covenant. The Council the same day unanimously approved the reports of the Committees of Thirteen and Six and referred the matter immediately to the Assembly.

Minister Wilson's fear that proclamation of the American embargo prior to the League decision would serve as an excuse for League inaction had proved to be unjustified. He reported from Geneva that the American proclamation had produced a "vivid impression," because the United States "had taken a position in respect to neutral rights which opened the way for the eventual application of a blockade and was, while neutral in law, in effect a sanction against Italy, owing to geographical accident."[24]

According to Article 16 of the Covenant, a unanimous condemnation by the League Council automatically and immediately brought about "the severance of all trade or financial relations, the prohibition of all intercourse between their nationals and the nationals of the Covenant-breaking State, and the prevention of all financial, commercial, or personal intercourse between the nationals of any other State, whether a Member of the League or not." Under amendments to the Covenant that had failed of ratification but which the Assembly had nevertheless recommended as procedural rules for implementing Article 16, the Council had the authority to restore peace by economic pressure and to notify members of the measures it recommended. These rules were intended primarily to allow the Council to coordinate actions of League members and to prevent confusion, but they could also be construed in such a way as to permit members to bypass the supposedly automatic and complete application of Article 16.

As the outbreak of war became imminent during September, the Assembly had adjourned its session so that it could meet again quickly. At the call of President Beneš it reconvened on October 9 to consider the Council's reports condemning Italy. Although Italy and its three friends, Albania, Austria, and Hungary, prevented the required unanimity, the Assembly on October 10 voted 50 to 1, with three abstentions, to establish an informal Coordination Committee to discuss and coordinate sanctions.[25]

The Coordination Committee met October 11 and established a smaller working group, a committee of 18 members. No one favored literal adherence to the obligations of Article 16. League members wished to proceed carefully and deliberately in the application of sanctions for the first time in history. Moreover, in order to have effective sanctions, the League needed a practical and politic way of preventing interchange between Italy and important nonmember countries like the United States, Germany, Japan, and Brazil.

In the task of coordinating sanctions, the Committee had to consider the attitude of League members toward the Italo-Ethiopian crisis: League members thought, or wanted to think, that the war would not last long. Italy, some contended, was on the verge of economic collapse and could hardly carry on a protracted war. Others argued that Mussolini wanted only a quick victory to avenge the humiliating defeat at Adowa in 1896 and to gain a little colonial glory. Therefore, many League members urged limited sanctions that would not lead to war and thus would not alienate Mussolini. Italy would compromise, they argued, and thus would save the prestige of the League, the face of Il Duce, and the Stresa front.

The proposals approved by the Coordination Committee and recommended to the participating states reflected the influence of these considerations. The Committee's Proposal One, which became the first sanction, prohibited the export to Italy of arms, ammunition, and implements of war and received immediate approval on October 11. It corresponded with the American embargo list, mostly because the American list had been based on the one contained in the Geneva Arms Traffic Convention of 1925. Both the League members and the United States had thus denied Italy actual military arms and supplies, but Ethiopia would theoretically remain free to purchase them from League members. No one, however, made a special effort to facilitate such purchases or to loan Ethiopia sufficient funds. Proposal One, therefore, hardly restricted Italy, which could manufacture its own armaments, and gave no encouragement to Ethiopia, which could not.

Proposals Two and Three set forth long-term sanctions designed to eliminate sources of cash and hard money by denying loans and credits to Italians and by prohibiting the importation of Italian products into member countries. Only so long as Italy had foreign exchange could it import nonembargoed raw materials and manufactured goods. In view of the drain on Italy's already poor economy by the depression and by excessive military expenditures, the Committee thought that these long-term proposals would diminish the Italian desire and capacity to fight and would thus compel Italy to compromise.

Proposal Four prohibited the exportation to Italy of certain raw materials, but only those whose production was in large part controlled by states that supported sanctions. It did not include strategic commodities like oil and cotton, which were scarce in Italy, because Italy could import these from nonmember states like the United States, which controlled significant quantities. Such trade with nonmembers would only negate League sanctions and divert permanent trade from members. It seemed more practical to restrict the embargo on raw materials, to wait to see how the simpler and less dangerous sanctions operated in practice, and to learn in what ways nonmember states might cooperate.[26]

The crucial decision to avoid sanctions that might lead to war had been made in mid-September by Hoare and Laval. Under Anglo-French leadership the Coordination Committee had restricted the embargo to those raw materials that were controlled by League members. However, in mid-October, when the Coordination Committee was determining this first round of sanctions, the Italian forces in East Africa had only a two-month supply of oil. With American cooperation, an embargo by the League covering oil might have rapidly halted Italy's war effort.[27]

Similarly, the first Hoare-Laval agreement had ruled out a naval blockade or the closure of the Suez Canal. If these measures had been effected, they not only would have halted Italian oil shipments to East Africa but also would have blocked all transportation between the Italian army in Ethiopia and the Italian government in Rome. As in the case of an oil embargo with American cooperation, Mussolini would have had the choice of seizing what territory he could and suing for a compromise or of striking out hopelessly at his alleged persecutors. Moreover, whereas an oil embargo would have required positive American cooperation, a naval blockade or closure of the Suez Canal could have been handled entirely by the League, with only American acquiescence—which Roosevelt had already given when he stated that the United States would not protect American citizens who sought to obtain war profits by trading with belligerents.[28]

But neither Great Britain nor the League ever seriously considered a naval blockade or the closure of the Suez Canal. Both measures seemed risky to Great Britain because they required positive action and enforcement by the British fleet. Among the possible direct sanctions, Britain preferred an oil embargo, which it could enforce in its own territory without threatening violence against Italian citizens, ships, or trade; if Italy objected, the Italian government would have to cast the first stone.

Winston Churchill commented wistfully after World War II that "a bold decision would have cut the Italian communications with Ethiopia" and that Great Britain would have been "successful in any naval battle which might have followed." He concluded that if ever there was an opportunity for "striking a decisive blow in a generous cause with the minimum of risk," this was it.[29]

Chapter Seven

The United States and the
Extension of Sanctions

The extension of League sanctions to such critical raw materials as oil, cotton, and copper would make the attitude of the United States toward embargoes particularly crucial. America produced enough of these raw materials to supply nearly all of Italy's requirements. If the United States wished to permit trade with Italy, it would definitely frustrate the action of the League. During the fall of 1935, therefore, other nations continually inquired about the American position, and the State Department tried to demonstrate that the United States policy was independent but nevertheless cooperative.

Did the government have authority to extend the embargo on arms, ammunition, and implements of war to include raw materials? Would the embargo apply to states drawn into the war by their support of the League Covenant? The State Department's response to these questions was ambiguous: The neutrality resolution did not specifically mention raw materials, but the government could not forecast policy in hypothetical situations. The State Department reminded more persistent questioners, however, that the President in his October 5 warning had used the words "in these specific circumstances." The government sought to indicate without actually saying so that it might extend the embargo, but that such an embargo would still apply only to Italy and Ethiopia.[1]

While the State Department hinted that the embargo would not apply to additional states involved in the conflict as a result of their League responsibilities, rumors to the contrary raised further questions about American policy. Ambassador Long in Rome observed to the foreign editor of *La Tribuna* that "in case the conflict should be enlarged the law as it now stands would enforce neutrality upon the United States in its relations with other belligerents." The United States, Long said, would apply neutrality embargoes even against Great Britain.[2] Near Eastern Affairs Chief Murray, who remembered an earlier communication in which Long had predicted an Anglo-Italian clash and urged strict American neutrality,[3] became worried that Long had misinterpreted the government's policy. The State Department certainly would not want Italy to suppose that the United States would apply the neutrality embargo to Great Britain if the enforcement of sanctions brought the British into the war. Hull immediately warned Long against forecasting government policy.*

The continual discussion of what American policy would be in the future annoyed Hull. He was especially vexed by rumors in the press and in communications from American diplomats in Geneva that the League intended to invite nonmembers to participate in sanctions, and that the United States had established a closer relationship with the League of Nations. Hull feared that such rumors might make it impossible for him to avoid a public statement about whether or not the United States would cooperate with the League in punishing the aggressor. A statement of cooperation would lead to a direct and losing clash with the isolationists, who would succeed even further in tying the hands of the Executive branch in matters of foreign policy. On the other hand, a refusal to cooperate would discourage the League, which might then shift the responsibility for failure to halt Italy to the United States.[4]

The only way Hull could maintain control over foreign policy and at the same time support those nations trying to preserve

---

* Memorandum by Murray, October 15, 1935; Long to Hull, October 16, 1935. Commenting on Long's indiscretion, the President's secretary, Louis M. Howe, wired Roosevelt on his cruise that Long "has been hypnotized by Mussolini and is sending five or six cables a day, little short of absolute Italian propaganda, and has given one interview which was highly indiscreet." (Howe to Roosevelt, October 18, 1935, Roosevelt Library.)

peace was to avoid pointed and embarrassing questions and to pursue the apparently independent foreign policy of refusing to assist belligerent nations in their war efforts. This course would not only appeal to pacifists, peace groups, and revisionists, who opposed American involvement in foreign problems and favored the reduction of war profits, but would also allow Hull some freedom in restricting trade with belligerents and thus indirectly some freedom in cooperating with the League.[5]

The Committee of Coordination, in part because of discreet suggestions by Wilson and Gilbert in Geneva, had apparently dropped the question of an invitation to the United States to participate in League sanctions. But the League was still considering making some approach to nonmembers. Gilbert notified Hull on October 15 that the Committee might send the records of its proceedings to Washington and ask for a reply. Gilbert feared that even a simple acknowledgement of receipt might create a misinterpretation at home and thus limit further American policy, or that a negative response might discourage the League.[6]

Hull, in replying to the Consul in Geneva two days later, reemphasized the need for an independent American policy but did not indicate his reaction to the idea of receiving the records of the Committee of Coordination. He said that he had "consciously calculated" American actions to assist in discouraging war: "The numerous acts and utterances of this Government," he explained, "both before and after the outbreak of hostilities, offer a definite and clear index of the course and attitude of this Government relative to the Italo-Ethiopian controversy in the future." It should be clear, however, Hull concluded, "that this Government is acting upon its own initiative and proceeding separately and independently of all other Governments or peace organizations."[7]

On October 18, as the Coordination Committee was finishing its initial work and had approved the first four recommendations of sanctions, Wilson telephoned Hull to ask if the Secretary would prefer that the Committee not send him any form of communication whatsoever. Hull replied that he only meant to be cautious, that he certainly did not wish to join issue with the League, and that he thought both the League and the United States should follow their own independent policies. "You understand," he said, "that we can go along on our course here, which nobody can take exception to at home or abroad, and prosecute it much more effectively if somebody from abroad is not pumping into us public inquiries, to make it appear we are being——"; at this point, Wilson interrupted, saying that the Committee would never pose the direct question, "Will you or won't you?" Hull reiterated the necessity of maintaining the pretense of an independent American policy, and Wilson concluded: "I think they understand that and very much appreciate your position already."[8]

Three days later Wilson forwarded a note from the President of the Coordination Committee transmitting its recommendations to non-League members. "I am instructed to add," Vasconcellos wrote, "that the Governments represented on the Coordination Committee would welcome any communication which any non-member state may deem it proper to make to me or notifications of any action which it may be taking in the circumstances."[9] The League had not openly requested American cooperation in the program of sanctions but it nevertheless showed lively interest in the reply.

In making its reply to Vasconcellos, the State Department had to consider that a noncommittal response would encourage Mussolini because it would indicate that the entire world did not condemn him. Such a reply might also provide hesitant League members with an excuse not to apply sanctions. The United States had passed judgment on Europe so often, *New York Times* correspondent Clarence K. Streit commented, that failure to do so now would strike the League a severe blow. At the very least, the League hoped for moral support.[10] Stanley K. Hornbeck, Chief of the Division of Far Eastern Affairs, referred specifically to Streit's article when he emphasized the importance of the American reply. Remembering the Manchurian crisis, Hornbeck urged that the United States give a clear indication of its sympathy for the League or at least declare that it would not place obstacles in the League's path. He suggested further that the administration seek from Congress greater discretionary authority for action paralleling League policies. A prompt and sympathetic reply would encourage Great Britain and France and would discourage Italy.[11]

Hull, with Roosevelt's approval, thanked Vasconcellos for the documents, mentioned the actions the United States had taken to prevent the war and to discourage its continuance, and concluded that the United States "views with sympathetic interest the individual or concerted efforts of other nations to preserve peace or to localize and shorten the duration of the war." The Secretary had thus stressed the peaceful aims of American policy while at the same time implicitly expressing the government's sympathy with the League of Nations.[12]

The *New York Times* correspondent in Geneva reported that the United States had disappointed League circles in failing to distinguish between aggressor and victim, but that nevertheless no one had expected America to adopt the League policy outright. "Officials here," reported the correspondent, "had been convinced by their American sources of information that the Administration was at heart with the League in its judgment and action and was striving to go as far to help and not hinder the League as the Neutrality Act, political situation, and popular desire to keep out of this war at any price permitted." They interpreted Hull's reply, therefore, as favorable to the League and assumed that he had done all that he could and had left the door open for further cooperation.[13]

The list of arms, ammunition, and implements of war proclaimed by President Roosevelt on September 25 included only articles for indisputable military use, and the embargo proclamation of October 5 prohibited their export to both Italy and Ethiopia. Yet the State Department had made it clear in interdepartmental memoranda, in a cabinet meeting, and in off-the-record comments to reporters that new developments might reopen the question.

Shortly after the outbreak of hostilities in October, Roosevelt suggested to Hull that the State Department "study carefully possible future additions to the list including such things as processed copper and steel so as to be ready to make decision" in case the League or Great Britain and France added articles of commerce not on the United States munitions list. Hull responded the next day with a definitive memorandum by Assistant Secretary R. Walton Moore, who pointed out that the courts would probably decide that the terms arms, ammunition, and implements of war had a commonly recognized and limited meaning. If in doubt, Moore continued, the judges would seek to determine the intent of Congress, as expressed during debate on the neutrality resolution. Moore noted that when a senator asked Key Pittman, Chairman of the Senate Foreign Relations Committee and sponsor of the resolution, whether implements of war included such commodities as wheat, corn, and cotton, Pittman had replied that neither he nor the Committee believed they did. The definition of implements of war, said Pittman, "is very generally recognized in international law. It is matter of fact that at this very session the Senate ratified a treaty or convention dealing with arms and implements of war in which they were categorically described." On the basis of Moore's memorandum, Hull reluctantly advised Roosevelt that the joint resolution did not give authority to extend the embargo to raw materials.[14]

Newspapers like the *New York Times* and prominent citizens like former Secretary of State Henry L. Stimson, however, strongly urged that the State Department interpret the neutrality resolution to include raw materials. The *New York Times* insisted that moral exhortation alone would not shut off trade in essential raw materials and that the United States would bear the responsibility if League sanctions failed. It did not care what Congress intended; the President, the *Times* pleaded, should take advantage of the opportunity "to act as it is understood the League would be glad to have him do."[15]

Although the administration had determined reluctantly that it had insufficient power to embargo raw materials, it deliberately never made this decision public. Several times reporters asked Hull if he had made a final determination, but he replied noncommittally that "every phase of that problem is receiving fullest attention from day to day and week to week. I have no further announcement on the subject to make at present." The President himself explained the administration's difficult decision in a personal letter. Under normal circumstances, Roosevelt pointed out, wheat and cotton and copper are not implements of war. "The letter of the law does not say so," he said, "and the trouble is that the spirit of the law, as shown by the debates during its passage, does not allow me to stretch it that far out—no matter how worthy the case."[16]

Congress had adjourned in late August and would not meet again until January. Since Congress had viewed presidential discretion and international cooperation with suspicion, the administration welcomed this recess. It would have an opportunity to use powers peculiar to the Presidency and because there would be time for public opinion to mount against the Italian aggression, the administration could hope to secure more satisfactory neutrality legislation in January.[17]

The Executive's principal weapon was the moral embargo, by which the President and the Secretary of State appealed to private citizens to effect by voluntary means what the government could not effect by law—the embargo on raw materials to belligerents. Hull favored a general appeal to the American people. Roosevelt, on the other hand, repeatedly suggested that the government make public the names of those who traded with Italy or traveled on Italian ships. If business with Italy had increased greatly, the administration undoubtedly would have used such a blacklist. But for the time being, Roosevelt acquiesced in Hull's view that "it would be wiser to proceed slowly. . . . A cooperative method with our public at the moment might probably have more beneficial results."[18]

In the statement accompanying his proclamation of the embargo on October 5, Roosevelt had warned that any American who traded with a belligerent did so at his own risk and should not expect government protection in case of trouble. Remembering the events of the First World War, most Americans did not object to the President's warning. New York importers and exporters, however, termed the banning of trade with Italy and Ethiopia "premature and ill-advised," and claimed it was a "serious blow" to New York and American commerce. Some criticized the President's statement, pointing out that Italian economic controls and foreign exchange shortages had already greatly reduced Italy's foreign trade. Others insisted on continuing trade with Italy on a cash basis as in the past. The Italian Commercial Attaché in New York encouraged businessmen to oppose the administration's policy by dangling the bait of a larger share of the Italian market in event of League sanctions.[19] Italian-Americans, who at the outset had displayed little interest in American policy, gradually realized that the moral embargo might seriously affect trade with Italy. *Il Progresso Italo-Americano,* the leading Fascist daily in the United States, at first relegated Roosevelt's embargo proclamations to the back page and dismissed them as "a mere formality"; but when New York exporters protested the government's policy, *Il Progresso* gave them front page headlines and top coverage all week.[20]

On October 10 Hull repeated Roosevelt's warning that private parties traded with belligerents at their own risk. He intended to counter the objections by New York businessmen and also to combat the impression created the previous day by Secretary of Commerce Roper, who had appeared to give a green light to exports to belligerents. Hull pointed out in a statement to the press that the law prohibited only the export of arms, ammunition, and implements of war, but that the President's warning "certainly was not intended to encourage transactions with the belligerents."[21]

Whatever certain business groups and Italian-American organizations thought about the neutrality policy followed by Roosevelt and Hull, most Americans approved it enthusiastically. It even received the support of some of the isolationists who had fought presidential discretion so vigorously. On October 16 Senator Nye wired Hull his "congratulations upon the spirit in which the neutrality policy laid down by Congress just before adjournment is being invoked in the face of pressure." Senator Vandenberg of Michigan applauded the new neutrality policy, even if it prevented the expression of the natural American sympathies in a given dispute or denied to America incidental commerce. In his statement about the policy, he concluded that there "seems to be an unfortunate disposition in some quarters to link our new neutrality formula with League of Nations sanctions. That was not the Congressional purpose and is not my conception of our formula."[22]

After issuing the embargo proclamations and the initial warnings about trade with belligerents, the State Department paused to consider its embargo policy again. "Our feeling," wrote James Dunn, Chief of the Division of Western European Affairs, "is that for the moment we are so far out ahead of the Geneva procedure that no particular action is required from us for the present. We are, however, watching intently every development and tendency in the situation."[23]

The State Department's Economic Adviser, Herbert Feis, suggested that the administration might pursue one of several alternatives with regard to trade with belligerents: (1) continuation of the present policy on the grounds that the President had no authority to do more; (2) reiteration in stronger terms of the undesirability of trade with belligerents on the basis that such trade ran counter to American neutrality, or, further, a statement that the government would pursue this policy of discouraging trade with belligerents pending an additional expression of Congressional opinion, or observation and recording of all transactions with belligerents, or, further, an announcement that the government would observe and record all transactions with belligerents and perhaps make public the names of those involved in such transactions; (3) redefinition of the neutrality resolution. The alternative that the administration would choose to follow, and the timing of its execution, would depend on the extent to which the administration intended to restrict trade with belligerents or to avoid thwarting the peace efforts of League members.[24]

The administration had already discarded the third alternative as legally impossible, and it considered the first alternative unacceptable as well, because it meant that trade in sanctioned raw materials would undoubtedly flourish and thus defeat the plans of the League. On October 20, therefore, both Roosevelt and Hull in separate and more strongly worded statements than they had made before reiterated the government's policy of discouraging trade with belligerents. They timed their statements, both of which the State Department prepared, for the eve of the reconvening of the Coordination Committee, which would resume consideration of sanctions and might propose the extension of sanctions to other, more important raw materials. They intended to reassure the League of Nations that the United States would cooperate by holding down exports of raw materials in one way or another. Roosevelt emphasized the determination of the United States "not to become involved in the controversy." He pointed out that in the course of war "tempting trade opportunities" might be offered to Americans "to supply materials which would prolong the war." But he did not think the American people would want "abnormally increased profits that temporarily might be secured by greatly extending" trade in such materials; nor would they want "the struggles on the battlefield to be prolonged because of profits accruing to a comparatively small number of American citizens." Hull's statement paralleled Roosevelt's: "The policy of this government to discourage dealings with the two belligerent nations . . . rests primarily upon the recent Neutrality Act designed to keep the nation out of war and upon the further purpose not to aid in protracting the war."[25]

Both statements insisted that the United States was determined to stay out of the war. But the President and Secretary of State still wished to cooperate with other nations in the effort to end the war. They hoped to show American cooperation by reducing trade with Italy and by indicating that the United States would not frustrate additional sanctions by the League. Domestic political exigencies required that American action, legal or moral, apply to the victim as well as to the aggressor. Whatever the lack of justice in the failure to distinguish between the two, it was important that the United States restrict the supplies it was sending to the aggressor. Because there was little actual or potential trade with Ethiopia, the administration had found room for maneuver; the more it limited trade with belligerents, the more it was cooperating with the League of Nations in imposing economic sanctions on Italy.

The statements of the President and the Secretary of State aimed at discouraging all trade with belligerents. But because the embargo was moral rather than legal in nature, the State Department realized that the government had no power to enforce it. Whenever a company inquired if the government would permit it to ship a certain commodity to Italy, the State Department responded ambiguously by sending copies of Roosevelt's and Hull's several statements on American policy. For example, on October 31, the day following the two press conferences, a representative of the Institute of American Meat Packers called at the State Department to find out what Roosevelt had meant by "abnormally increased profits" and to discover whether the government desired that all shipments to Italy cease. Joseph C. Green, Chief of the Office of Arms and Munitions Control, consulted other members of the Department, including Hull, before he replied that the government "particularly desired to minimize exports to Italy of manufactured products or raw materials which would serve a definitely military purpose." It "had no desire," he said, "to starve the Italian people," but he cautioned the Meat Packers' agent against entering into future commitments because "the situation was changing rapidly and the policy of this Government might be changed."[26]

Unwilling or unable to read between the lines, the Institute representative replied: "Permit me to comment amicably and respectfully that perusal of the letter still leaves me without knowledge as to the desires of our Government. . . . Is it not possible to indicate specifically exactly what the desires of the United States Government are?" Green answered in the only manner he could, that "it should be understood that any American citizen who voluntarily enters into any commercial transaction with either of the belligerents does so at his own risk."[27]

At Hull's press conference on October 31, correspondents wanted to know if the administration was considering any measures to restrict exports to belligerents in case the moral embargo proved insufficient, or if the administration made any distinction between normal trade with belligerents and trade resulting in abnormal profits. Hull replied that he had nothing to add since oral explanations of formal statements would lead only to more questions and further explanations. One correspondent then mentioned a *New York Times* interpretation that Hull's and Roosevelt's statements "were tantamount to declaring for the cessation of all American trade with Italy." Hull remarked that he found this interpretation quite interesting, whether it was true or not. The correspondent replied that this was precisely what he would like to know. Hull ended the exchange by refusing to discuss what the government's policy might be if American exporters supplied Italy with raw materials denied Italy by League members.[28]

President Roosevelt, too, refused to give a direct answer to questions asked by correspondents concerning a clarification of the administration's policy. Instead, he told the story of a mid-September visit by George F. Johnson, of the Endicott-Johnson Shoe Company, who had wanted advice on whether to fill a large order from the Italian government. "Were they ladies' slippers?" Roosevelt had asked facetiously. When he learned that the order called for heavy shoes worn by soldiers, Roosevelt had declared that he wouldn't take the contract if he owned the shoe company.[29]

Because the administration refused to commit itself, citizens and businessmen, as well as interested foreign governments, had to figure out for themselves whether it meant to discourage all trade or merely abnormal trade with belligerents, as well as what action it would take if its recommendations failed. The administration could not answer these questions because its powers of enforcement were so limited.[30]

In addition to the moral embargo, the administration used other methods of demonstrating its desire not to impede the collective efforts of the League. For example, at the direct request of the State Department, Secretary of the Treasury Henry Morgenthau canceled his scheduled return from Europe on the Italian Line.[31] Hull instructed Ambassador Long in Rome and Chargé Engert in Addis Ababa to suspend all publicity activities in connection with the usual consular trade promotion. They should tell all inquirers that in accordance with the government's policy leaving individuals to trade at their own risk, the State Department would not assist American commerce or travel in belligerent countries.[32]

A West Coast labor leader wired Hull on November 16 that the steamer *Oregon,* loaded with a cargo of gas, was preparing to depart, apparently for Italian Somaliland. He stated that he would hold the vessel in port until promised "by the United States State Department that full protection will be guaranteed members of our organization who are members of the crew." Hull wired back that if "the gasoline mentioned . . . is in fact destined to an Italian possession, no such guarantee as you suggest can be given."[33] The Federal Reserve Bank kept a constant check on all banks granting credit to Italian firms. The Department of Commerce informed the State Department daily on import-export trade with belligerents, and Under Secretary Phillips sent Roosevelt a regular copy of the reports. The President himself had recommended the latter two activities, and he also continually urged Hull to make public the names of violators of the administration's trade policy. In his press statement of October 30, Roosevelt clearly implied a threat to wield a big stick, if necessary, to enforce the embargo.[34]

The question of Egyptian participation in sanctions provided another opportunity for the use of Executive powers to encourage effective action by the League. The United States, Italy, and several League powers had capitulatory rights in Egypt which gave special protections to foreign commerce and citizens. If Egypt applied sanctions against Italy, some American businesses might initiate or continue a lucrative trade with Italy in essential and sanctioned supplies. If the United States were to insist upon its full capitulatory rights, the American flag would protect trade with Italy and frustrate Egyptian cooperation with the League.

In view of the President's statements and the government's policy of discouraging trade with belligerents, Consul James R. Childs recommended that the State Department authorize its representatives in Egypt to refrain from asserting capitulatory rights on behalf of American citizens trading with either belligerent. Childs pointed out that besides being in line with American policy, the refusal to use these rights would protect the United States in the future if a scapegoat had to be found.[35] Near Eastern Affairs Division Chief Murray agreed with Childs, noting that "General Motors has already made large shipments to Italian East Africa and possibly may be tempted to continue this lucrative trade which has been carried on through Egypt." The State Department authorized its diplomatic and consular agents in Egypt to refrain from assisting American citizens who encountered difficulties trading with a belligerent.[36]

Italians were greatly relieved that the application of the American embargo had not singled out Italy for moral condemnation and had not included vital raw materials. The Italian press continually reassured its readers of American neutrality. Reports from Italian correspondents in the United States stressed the patriotic activities of Italian-Americans and the statements by isolationists that the United States would stay out of the conflict and would not cooperate with Great Britain or the League.[37]

Reading only the national press, Italians could have little idea of the extent to which the world condemned their country because of the invasion of Ethiopia. Even *New York Times* correspondent Anne O'Hare McCormick, who often tended to sympathize with Mussolini, noted that foreign news printed in Italy, "is headlined or suppressed as national feeling needs to be stirred up or toned down, while what opinion there is supporting the Italian stand is, of course, always featured." The quotations that Italian papers selected from American and other foreign newspapers, could readily lead a nonthinking reader to conclude that the "great body of foreign sentiment recognizes the justice of the Italian cause." But because a large number of foreign papers still circulated in Italy, Mrs. McCormick pointed out, educated Italians knew what the world thought; and from them some of the truth filtered through to almost everyone. Whatever the Italian press said about the American embargo as a measure of strict neutrality, the Italian people "instinctively recognized in the President's swift asperity a judgment on Italy and a reinforcement of the British determination to make sanctions work."[38]

Roosevelt's warnings against travel on belligerent ships and trade with warring nations particularly disturbed Italians. Although neither statement had the force of law, Italians were uneasy about the fact that the results would affect Italy far more than Ethiopia. Under Secretary Suvich in Rome speculated on the meaning of secret talks between British and American representatives in Geneva and Washington. Ambassador Rosso in Washington complained to Under Secretary William Phillips that American neutrality operated unequally on the belligerent parties and that the embargoes and proclamations affected only Italy. The State Department assured Rosso that this resulted from circumstances rather than from intent.[39]

American policy especially disturbed *La Tribuna*. Along with other Italian papers, it emphasized the protests of Italian-American groups and New York exporters. Asking what risk American citizens could face traveling on Italian ships, an editorial in *La Tribuna* pointed out that Ethiopia did not even possess the shadow of a ship. Such an unclear situation, the Rome daily concluded, certainly justified a protest.[40]

On October 10, in boldface type in the center of the front page, *La Tribuna* carried an editorial entitled "American Problems." It contrasted Hull's statement that America had acted independently of other powers and solely in application of its neutrality legislation with stories from Geneva that the British had obtained the indirect agreement of the United States to the program of sanctions. As an indication of this assent, *La Tribuna* pointed to the visits of respective ambassadors to foreign offices in London and Washington. Secretary of State Hull and the American government, the Italian newspaper concluded, had the duty of setting the record straight and not hiding behind excuses. Compared with the daily diatribes against Great Britain and the League, however, this criticism of the United States was mild.[41]

Rome hailed the cautious American response to the documents and recommendations of the League's Coordination Committee as a confirmation of American neutrality and a defeat for extremists who wanted the United States to participate in sanctions. The *New York Times* quoted an Italian spokesman as admitting that Italy could not help but be "gratified" at the reaffirmation of American neutrality and the consequent lack of world solidarity against Italy. Italians ignored or distorted the unfavorable aspects of Hull's reply. Indeed, they even revised the portion declaring that American policy would not assist in prolonging the war, and sought to show that America was withholding support from the League and abstaining from sanctions out of fear of lengthening the war.[42]

By the end of October 1935, the first round of League action in the Italo-Ethiopian crisis had concluded. The world organization had condemned Italy as an aggressor and had recommended a program of limited economic sanctions. The United States had sought to indicate, quite cautiously, that its sympathies lay with Ethiopia and the League and that it did not wish to frustrate the League program in any way. So far, the United States had not seriously offended Italy. Ambassador Rosso had advised his government that despite the American sympathy for Ethiopia, he did not think the United States would join in any sanctions against Italy.[43] Except for a few questions and protests, Italy had kept silent with regard to the United States. The crisis in Italian-American relations came in November, when the League considered a second round of more effective sanctions.

On October 31 the Coordination Committee met to consider the replies to its recommendations. According to American Consul Prentiss Gilbert in Geneva, the reaction to the proposals exceeded even the most hopeful estimate.[44] Because of the many favorable responses, the Committee was able to select a date, November 18, for the formal imposition upon Italy of the four proposed sanctions. Earlier in October the Canadian Delegate to the League had argued that only a comprehensive program of economic sanctions could be effective, and on November 3 he formally moved the application of an embargo on those basic raw materials not included in the fourth proposal. On November 6 the Coordination Committee approved in principle the extension of sanctions to vital raw materials such as oil and agreed to recommend implementation whenever it obtained sufficient pledges to ensure effective operation of the new embargo.

When the Coordination Committee spoke of obtaining sufficient pledges, it meant that it awaited the assurance of United States cooperation in an embargo on oil. The United States produced approximately 60 per cent of the world supply of oil, but in the first nine months of 1935 it was supplying only 6.3 per cent of Italy's oil imports. Quite obviously, if the League states prohibited their citizens from exporting oil to Italy or Italian Africa, the United States could easily expand its oil shipments to meet all Italian needs. If a nonmember state could frustrate a League sanction so readily, the sanction would be useless.

Roosevelt and Hull had intended the moral embargo to demonstrate that the United States would not obstruct the efforts of the League of Nations. They had timed their statements on October 30 to coincide with the reconvening of the Coordination Committee. Now that the Committee had approved in principle an extension of sanctions and had apparently left the final decision to the United States, the administration intensified its efforts to prevent the export of raw materials to Italy.

When American oil sales to Italy increased during the fall, the administration considered making a new appeal explicitly mentioning oil, both as a reassurance to the League and as a moral embargo on similar raw materials before the League imposed its own sanction.[45] Roosevelt predicted to Postmaster General James A. Farley at a White House luncheon on November 14 that the League meeting the following week would mark the start of a sanctions movement to cripple Italy. He said that he might have to publish a list of American firms shipping materials capable of military use to Italy. The President insisted to Farley, who was Democratic National Chairman as well as Postmaster General, that he knew he was "walking a tightrope" and that he realized "the seriousness of this from an international as well as a domestic point of view."[46]

On November 15 Hull issued an unusually sharp warning, listing specific raw materials, the export of which in abnormal quantities he labeled as decidedly against the administration's policy. This time Hull clearly meant not all trade with belligerents but only trade in abnormal quantities: "There are certain commodities," he said, "such as oil, copper, trucks, tractors, scrap iron, and scrap steel which are essential war materials, although not actually 'arms, ammunition, or implements of war.'" Noting an increase in the export of these for war purposes, Hull said this increase was directly "contrary to the policy of this Government as announced in official statements of the President and Secretary of State, as it is also contrary to the general spirit of the recent neutrality act."[47]

The distinction between normal and abnormal exports, now the basis for the administration's moral embargo, was derived from Hull's efforts during the First World War, when he was in the House of Representatives, to differentiate between peacetime and wartime profits.[48] Roosevelt had not favored such a distinction with regard to exports, having commented to Hull in October that he opposed "any quota system of exports to Italy," and that he thought the United States "must either allow an export item or disallow it as ammunition." But Roosevelt acquiesced in Hull's program just as he had given up his insistence to publicize the names of those who violated the moral embargo.[49] The two men worked together well; as long as domestic political problems did not intrude, Hull had a considerable amount of freedom to follow his own cautious but internationalist policy.

The exclusion of cotton as one of Hull's "essential war materials" raised eyebrows. Murray attributed this omission to domestic politics, but Hull denied that Southern representatives had exerted any pressure and insisted that he had excluded cotton because exports of it had dropped since 1934. He had listed only those articles exported to Italy in abnormal amounts; if cotton exports or those of any raw material exceeded substantially that of earlier years, he would include them as well. In effect, then, Hull added to his list of essential goods cotton and any other raw material that eventually might be exported to belligerents in abnormal amounts.[50]

Hull's moral embargo received the approval, in letter if not in spirit, of Senator Borah, the ranking Republican member of the

Senate Foreign Relations Committee. The Idaho isolationist interpreted the government's policy as one opposed to bringing
"pressure upon either of the belligerents." Holding exports to a
normal peacetime basis seemed to him a sensible course. He rea-
soned that "the primary purpose of our government is above all
things to stay out of European controversies, and to join League
sanctions would be to plunge us into European difficulties."[51] It
was good, Hull must have thought, to have Borah on his side for
a change, even if for the wrong reason.

As the State Department in November attempted to bolster the
not entirely successful moral embargo, the administration also
used other methods to restrict the export of vital raw materials to
Italy. One of these was to use the powers of the Shipping Board
Bureau of the Commerce Department. The Shipping Board could
grant or refuse permission for the transfer of American-registered
vessels to foreign ownership. At the advice of the State Department, for example, Italy could not buy the *U.S.S. San Diego* for
scrapping.[52] The Shipping Board had a particularly critical power
over mortgages. It could exert pressure on shipowners indebted to
it if they shipped raw materials to belligerents. In the case of a
mortgage in good standing that did not require an extension, the
government could do little, but it would have a whiphand in case
an owner sought funds for new construction or a renewal of the
mortgage. In depression times especially, this was a powerful
hold.[53]

In the case of the *U.S.S. Ulysses,* a privately owned oil tanker
with a $400,000 defaulted mortgage, the Secretary of Commerce
had deferred foreclosure proceedings because he had reason to
think the owner was paying the preservation costs himself and
might soon obtain business. But when the *Ulysses* obtained a contract to carry oil to Italy, the Shipping Board Bureau asked the
State Department's advice. Hull explained to Roosevelt that the
owner had spent a considerable amount of money in conditioning
the vessel for this contract; by foreclosing, the government might
be responsible for damages. Roosevelt nevertheless insisted that
the *Ulysses* not proceed with its cargo of oil for Italy. The State
Department, therefore, advised the Shipping Board on November
13 to foreclose the mortgage at once if the owner continued to
handle oil for Italy, but if he refrained, the government would
give him more time.[54]

On November 18 Ambassador Rosso revealed that the Italian government, through its Naval Attaché in Washington, had contracted for the purchase of oil to be shipped on the *Ulysses*.[55] Rosso complained to James Dunn, Western European Affairs Chief, that the Attaché had just received a telegram from the company saying that the American government had refused to permit that vessel to make the voyage. Rosso thought this clearly "an unfriendly act," which assisted the powers waging an unjustified economic war on Italy. Did the government, Rosso asked, intend to withhold permission for all shipments of oil to Italy? Dunn answered that "as far as the direct action of this government was concerned only those ships upon which the government held mortgages were involved."[56]

Dunn's answer considerably mollified the Ambassador. The Italian Embassy informed the contractor of the *Ulysses* that the "American Government has no objection to the shipment of fuel oil to Italian ports" if accomplished in vessels not under mortgage to the Shipping Board. When the report of this reached the State Department, Dunn called Rosso on November 18 to set the record straight. The United States certainly did object to shipments of oil to Italy, Dunn declared, and he cited the many statements made by Roosevelt and Hull to stress American policy on trade with belligerents. The key word in Dunn's reply to Rosso was "direct": The government could do nothing directly to prevent ships not under a Shipping Board mortgage from transporting raw materials to Italy, but this did not mean that the government approved it.[57]

In the meantime, the owner of the *Ulysses* claimed that he had spent $40,000 to prepare the vessel for the voyage, that he had signed the contract before the announcement of the government's policy on November 15, and that he now faced bankruptcy. The Shipping Board refused any additional advances of money. Finally, on the basis of equity, Assistant Secretary of State Moore recommended that the ship be freed and permitted to make its voyage; Roosevelt reluctantly approved the action.[58]

During October and November 1935 the United States government had clearly shown its good faith in attempting to restrict trade with Italy and thus to cooperate with the League's actual and proposed sanctions program. Not having the power to embargo raw materials or to discriminate between aggressor and victim, the administration had sought in other ways to achieve these goals. But as antisanctionists and lukewarm supporters of the League continually claimed, American trade with Italy in vital raw materials had increased despite the administration's policy. American commerce with Italy for the last three months of 1935 amounted to just under 20 per cent more than it had been for the same period the previous year.[59] The greatest increase was in oil shipments, particularly those made by small, independent companies. Without the administration's effort, however, trade with Italy undoubtedly would have increased much more.

The administration had committed itself to avoid thwarting the League's actions in restraining Italy, and had all but proclaimed publicly that if the League finally implemented Proposal Four A for an oil sanction, the United States would find a way to cooperate. The administration hoped that if the moral embargo failed in limiting American trade with belligerents to prewar quantities, and if it became evident that such trade by American businessmen was causing the defeat of sanctions, an outraged public would force recalcitrant companies to reform or would demand more effective legislation from Congress. A public opinion survey taken by *Fortune* in late 1935 showed a plurality (47.9 to 40.8 per cent) favoring economic pressure in cooperation with other nations to preserve international peace and morality.[60] The administration's hope did not reach a test, however, because events in Europe soon undermined its policy.

Haile Selassie realized that world sympathy and public opinion were strong factors in his support. Early in November, in a broadcast directed especially to the United States, he urged Americans to search their consciences and to associate their country with economic sanctions against Italy. The Emperor commented on his heavy mail from Americans expressing sympathy and asking what they could do to aid Ethiopia. Now that the League had united in a program of sanctions, he said, the time had come to answer his American friends and to urge them to join in support of sanctions against the violator of peace.[61]

Although Italy was beginning to fear that the United States might join in League sanctions, as Haile Selassie was appealing for it to do, Ambassador Long reported in early November that the atmosphere in Italy still continued to be friendly to America. He even expected that Italian anger against Great Britain and other League members would lead Italy to seek more trade with the United States. Because of the controlled Italian press, the average Italian, Long thought, had no knowledge of the intricacies of American policy. But he added that "the Government and the well-informed view the attitude of America with considerable suspicion and are as yet unable to make up their minds that the United States will not proceed further on the road to support the policies adopted at Geneva."[62]

In spite of the increased concern among Italians about American policy, the statements by Roosevelt and Hull on October 30 received little comment in the Italian press or from Italian diplomats. Suvich wondered if they portended a change in the American neutrality policy, but he did not pursue the point.[63] La Stampa argued that although Hull's statements furnished evidence of the infiltration of British propaganda, the United States was nevertheless strictly observing its neutrality declaration. Foreign Office spokesman Virginio Gayda suggested in a long editorial on "Sanctions and the Americas" that "the Americans do not intend to set themselves up as judges and executioners of European countries, for they do not intend to encourage European interference in their affairs," and concluded that the deepest reasons for American abstention were "an honest comprehension of Italian needs, a grander interpretation of the duties of civilization, and a proud independent judgment."[64] These statements were not naïve; government circles understood the intentions behind American policy, but they preferred to remain silent so long as the United States did nothing active to implement it.

Hull's press statement of November 15 placing a moral embargo on vital raw materials such as oil marked a turning point in Italian-American relations. The United States now seemed to be on the verge of joining the League sanctionist states.[65] Under Secretary Suvich complained on November 20 that Hull's statement amounted to a sharp departure from the strict neutrality that Italy had hoped for, and that it gave the definite impression of cooperation with the League. The next day Long commented to Hull that even if the Secretary thought American policy independent from League policy, no one else did: "I appreciate the position in which you find yourself," said Long, "in regard to your desire not to vitiate the action of other governments on the application of sanctions," but this policy might cause an abrupt reversal in Italian-American relations because the average Italian simply would not expect it. Long wrote in his diary that he thought the administration's policy would make possible a League embargo on oil that would force Italy to retaliate and thus bring on a European war. He believed that a European struggle could be avoided if the Italo-Ethiopian war were allowed to drag on until Italy wasted its resources and had to compromise.[66]

On November 22 Ambassador Rosso, following instructions from Rome, called on Hull and stated without reservation his government's belief that the official declarations and public statements made by American officials during the past several months, especially Hull's statement of November 15, constituted "an extension and aggravation, to the principal detriment of Italy" of the neutrality resolution. In addition, he complained that these statements violated the Italian-American Treaty of 1871, which guaranteed "complete freedom of commerce and navigation" to both countries. He argued that if the United States applied a limitation on the export of raw materials, as Hull envisaged, it would "assume the meaning of a 'sanction' and therefore the positive character of an unfriendly act."[67]

Hull began his long and exasperated answer by assuring Rosso that "the people of this country today do not feel personally unfriendly towards the people of Italy." As a result of the "extremely disastrous and unsatisfactory experience" of the First World War, however, he said, Americans "are vigorously and almost wildly against war." Hull reminded Rosso that Italy owed millions of dollars to the United States from the previous war and that many Americans thought he should "demand aggressively, if necessary, payment by the Italian Government of this indebtedness instead of spending hundreds of millions in this Ethiopian conquest."

American policy, Hull contended, aimed at keeping out of the war, but the United States also wished to maintain world peace. Hull thought it "really astonishing" to find that a government could not follow such a policy "without being attacked and a demand made to supply war materials to a belligerent under penalty of being charged with an unfriendly act." To Rosso's complaint that the way in which the administration conducted its neutrality policy discriminated against Italy, Hull pointed out that the embargo denied war materials to both Italy and Ethiopia and thus placed both belligerents "as nearly on a parity in this respect as it is possible for them to be. The charge of discrimination, therefore, does not apply."

Hull repeatedly asked why Italy did not "sit down with others and work out this difficulty in a peaceful manner" in view of the "awful repercussions" in the rest of the world. He referred specifically to the Far East, where Japan was taking advantage of the European preoccupation with the Italo-Ethiopian conflict to encroach further upon China. Hull reminded Rosso that he and the President had "pleaded and almost prayed with Mr. Mussolini" not to start another war, but that the Italian leader had ignored the pleas and then expected the United States to "furnish him with war supplies while he prosecutes the war ad libitum."

Furthermore, Hull pointed out, simply because similarities existed between the League sanctions program and the American neutrality policy, the United States could not be charged with unneutrality and unfriendliness. Hull insisted, with something less than candor, that his November 15 statement announcing a moral embargo on vital raw materials had no connection with the plans of the League. When Rosso referred to the oil sanction that he said the League would impose at the end of the month, Hull said weakly that that remained to be seen.

Hull's outburst shook Rosso severely and left him "very much flushed."[68] If Rosso reported the full extent of this interview to Rome, Mussolini must have realized that Hull had meant what he said in his earlier statements. Italy could not count on American supplies of oil and other raw materials in the more and more likely event of an extended League of Nations embargo. Hull's emphatic lecture to Rosso may have been an important factor in Mussolini's threat to break the Franco-Italian alliance, which followed shortly thereafter, causing the abrupt postponement of the November 29 meeting of the Coordination Committee to consider the implementation of the oil embargo.

Roosevelt congratulated Hull on his "classic" clash with Rosso. "You did a splendid job," he said, "of making our position clear and, at the same time, pointing out the very untenable position in which Italy has deliberately placed herself." The President added that he did not think the language of the Italian-American Treaty of 1871 covered a situation in which one of the signatories launched an invasion.[69]

The Italian press, however, still did not alter its standard procedure of citing expressions of American public opinion that favored or could appear to favor Italian policy. One article actually began with the statement, "Some noteworthy expressions in favor of the Italian point of view appeared yesterday evening," and then cited remarks by various individuals, including Father Coughlin and Norman Thomas.[70] But other viewpoints were also emerging, though Italian newspapers always explained that the American public did not support the administration or that, if it did in part, British propaganda had caused the deception. *La Tribuna*'s London correspondent wrote that the attitude of the administration justified the highest hopes of the sanctionists, but that despite Roosevelt's and Hull's "goodwill" the moral embargo was impractical and an oil embargo unconstitutional.[71] *Il Corriere della Sera* wanted to know "how many times Roosevelt has confused his own personal opinion with that of the better and more enlightened part of the American people." Despite the growing "reaction to pro-League manifestations of some American leaders," *La Tribuna* noted that British agents continued to swarm about Washington seeking to obtain American support for the League.[72]

The climax of the Italo-Ethiopian crisis, if not its conclusion, was fast approaching. The administration had withstood the pressure of Italian-American and export groups and, indeed, had won considerable popular support for its effort to keep the United States out of the war. At the same time the administration had indicated clearly that it would find some method of cooperation so as not to frustrate whatever further action the League of Nations might decide upon. The Committee of Coordination was scheduled to meet on November 29, at which time it might formally impose an oil sanction, which it had already approved in principle. Italy feared the application of this oil sanction because it might effectively stall the highly mechanized Italian Army and thereby end the Italo-Ethiopian War.

Chapter Eight

Great Britain, the Extension of Sanctions, and the Hoare-Laval Plan

Great Britain had been reluctant early in 1935 to indicate that it would defend the Covenant of the League of Nations, but British public opinion, outraged by Italy's arrogance and defiance, compelled the cautious government to assume leadership of the League in condemning Italy. The League had applied a first round of limited economic sanctions and now was considering a second and much more effective series of punitive trade restrictions, the most important of which was a sanction on vital raw materials such as oil.

The British government was not at all eager to lead the League into imposing an oil sanction. It placed little confidence in the League as a method of settling international controversies and preferred more traditional diplomatic ways. In particular, the Conservative leaders feared a German revival in Europe more than they disliked an Italian colonial conquest in Africa, and therefore hoped to maintain Italian friendship against the potential German threat. To rationalize their wish to avoid offending Italy, Conservatives continually pointed out that Britain was not the sole producer or transporter of oil products; an effective oil embargo would require not only American assistance, but also the cooperation of several important oil-producing League states—the Netherlands, Rumania, the Soviet Union, and Venezuela.

It did not seem likely, however, that any of these states would oppose an oil sanction. Venezuela, like the United States, theoretically could divert large shipments of oil to Italy if it chose to do so, but because of its political instability, the Venezuelan government had avoided a positive stand. (In any event, other League states largely controlled the refining and transportation of Venezuelan oil.) The Netherlands, Rumania, and the Soviet Union, which together had supplied approximately 75 per cent of Italian oil imports during the first nine months of 1935, had supported League sanctions and announced their willingness to impose an oil embargo if other producers agreed.[1] Public opinion in the Netherlands, just as in Great Britain, condemned the Italian invasion. Rumania, despite its profitable trade with Italy in oil and other products, would not obstruct increased League sanctions against Italy; Rumania's primary concern was to defend the League as the guarantor of the First World War peace settlement, which had rewarded Rumania at the expense of Hungary.

The Soviet Union was primarily interested in League action against Italy as a precedent that might deter Germany in the future. In September 1934, because of the increasing threat posed by Nazi Germany, Russia had joined the League, which it had formerly regarded with suspicion as an imperialist organization. From the time of Hitler's assumption of power in 1933 and Germany's withdrawal from Geneva, Soviet foreign policy had concentrated on preventing a struggle with the Nazis. In late November 1935, when the League appeared ready to take definite action against Italy, Russia therefore announced its willingness to proceed with an embargo on raw materials such as oil, in the hope that "unity of action will . . . put a check on all future attempts—from whatever quarter they may come—to disturb peace by attacks on the world's most crucial spots."[2]

Yet even with the support of other oil-producing states in the League, Great Britain was reluctant to press for an oil sanction. The United States, as well, had indicated that it would cooperate as best it could with a League program. But the British still hesitated to take a definite stand. British confidence in securing the cooperation of the United States seemed to correspond to the degree of British sympathy with the League and the proposed action against Italy. Right-wing Conservatives, who were strong in the House of Lords and prominent in the British press, strongly objected to sanctions against "friendly Italy" and opposed the League of Nations, often calling it nothing more than a debating society. American cooperation, they insisted, was a chimera.[3]

But the majority of both government and opposition leaders in Great Britain agreed that an oil sanction would be effective and that the United States would probably cooperate with it. The Liberal and Labour parties demanded an immediate oil embargo and bitterly criticized the government for winning the November 14 election on what they called the "false pretense" of promising an immediate embargo. The Conservative government, on the other hand, was prepared to implement an oil sanction if absolutely necessary, but it was much more interested in finding a way to compromise with Italy.

Hugh Dalton, Undersecretary for Foreign Affairs in an earlier Labour government and the party spokesman on foreign affairs in the critical debate in Parliament on December 5, 1935, charged the Conservative government with neglecting its duty. Although the United States had not joined the League, Dalton said, it was showing signs of "willingness to join in putting pressure upon their own oil interests in various ways, financially and otherwise, providing those who are members of the League will themselves stand up to this question and impose the oil sanction." If the British government would not take the leadership, he declared, it would assume responsibility "for the continuance of the war and for a weakening of the collective peace system."[4]

The *Daily Herald,* the organ of the Labour party, claimed that advocacy of an oil sanction would do honor to Britain and argued that even without American cooperation an oil embargo would make it hard for the Italians to continue the war. But it added that "American cooperation is by no means unlikely."[5] The Liberal *News-Chronicle,* not quite so restrained, asked how Great Britain could pretend to support the sanctions policy of the League of Nations and yet leave it to a non-League state to enforce the most elementary of all sanctions. "The facts are," declared the *News-Chronicle,* "that President Roosevelt is notoriously occupied at the moment with the consideration of means to check the export of war materials to Italy."[6]

The British government, more cautious than the two principal opposition parties, supported sanctions only reluctantly. Its principal spokesmen on foreign affairs agreed that American expressions of intent to cooperate made an oil sanction practicable, if it became necessary. To an unusual extent, Foreign Secretary Hoare determined British policy, and the Cabinet rarely challenged his ideas. Prime Minister Baldwin showed little interest in foreign affairs and allowed Hoare a relatively free hand.[7] Hoare's assistant, the Minister for League of Nations Affairs, Anthony Eden, made an impressive appearance in Geneva but he had little influence on the ultimate determination of British foreign policy in London. The only member of the government besides Hoare who played a major role in formulating foreign policy was Neville Chamberlain, the Chancellor of the Exchequer.

During the parliamentary debate on adjournment prior to the November 14 general election, Hoare boasted that the first round of economic sanctions would effectively check Italy: "If it is collectively applied," he said, "and the States that are not members of the League do not attempt to frustrate it—and I have no reason to think that they will frustrate it—it will definitely shorten the duration of the war."[8]

On December 5, as Parliament met following the government's electoral victory, Hoare reiterated that Great Britain would do its share in an oil embargo as it had in the whole League program of collective action. Since the previous session of the House of Commons, the League had approved in principle a second round of sanctions, including an embargo on vital raw materials such as oil. But "the question still to be decided," said Hoare, "is whether the action of the non-member states would render ineffective the action of the member states. Further light has recently been thrown upon this very important question, with the result that it is now possible for the Committee of Eighteen to have a further meeting for the purpose of discussing the actual application of a form of pressure that has already been accepted in principle."[9] In this statement, Hoare could only have been referring to the efforts of the United States to restrict trade with belligerents and in particular to Hull's statement of November 15 applying the moral embargo to oil. The sanctionist *News-Chronicle* considered this "the most important passage" of Hoare's speech and cited it as clear proof that the British government was satisfied that the action of non-member states would not make the decisions of the League ineffective. "America, in plain English," the *News-Chronicle* concluded, "will not supply Italy with the oil of which the League's embargo will deprive her."[10]

Later in December, when Hoare had to explain the failure of his attempt to reach an agreement with Italy, he did not say that he had pursued this compromise policy because he had anticipated an American refusal to cooperate. Instead he specifically alluded to his fear that nonmembers would indeed cooperate with the League and that their cooperation would make an oil embargo effective, which might therefore cause Italy to retaliate with a military attack. "About a fortnight ago," Hoare explained, "it was clear that a new situation was about to be created by the question of the oil embargo. It seemed clear that, supposing an oil embargo were to be imposed and that the non-member states took an effective part in it, the oil embargo might have such an effect upon the hostilities [in Africa] as to force their termination." Anglo-Italian relations immediately became more dangerous, Hoare continued, and Great Britain had received reports from all sides that "Italy would regard the oil embargo as a military sanction or an act involving war against her."[11]

Neville Chamberlain agreed with Hoare that the League would reach the critical point in its efforts to end the Italo-Ethiopian war when the Committee met to consider the oil sanction. Chamberlain thought that the decision to impose further sanctions "really turned on the possibility of making the oil embargo effective." He believed that the United States had already gone further than usual in its assurances of cooperation, and that consequently, the question of an oil sanction was being taken seriously. Although Chamberlain would have preferred that someone else take the lead, he believed that as a last resort Great Britain ought to do so: "If we backed out now because of Mussolini's threats," Chamberlain argued, "we should leave the Americans in the air." If this happened, he went on, the United States might "decline in the future to help us in any way, sanctions would crumble, the League would lose its coherence, and our whole policy would be destroyed." Chamberlain obviously believed that the United States would cooperate.[12]

The Times, a strong supporter of the government, thought the attitude of the United States would "have an important effect in helping to shorten the conflict." Noting that Roosevelt and Hull had acted even before the League members, *The Times* argued that the United States had "endeavored in successive declarations to discourage American trade with both belligerents" and that these declarations were not being allowed to remain merely the expression of a platonic sentiment." Although *The Times* saw no collusion or direct cooperation between Washington and Geneva, it did conclude that the discouragement of the export of oil and other materials of war would "make practicable the prohibition by the League Powers of the supply of oil to Italy." In the same way, *The Times* concluded, prohibition of oil shipments by the League would "help the President to make his discouragement effective."[13] The diplomatic correspondent of the Conservative *Daily Telegraph* stated emphatically that as a result of the warnings of Roosevelt and Hull to exporters, "it has appeared that the oil pipeline to Italy could be seriously blocked, if not completely closed. . . . A decision by the League states to apply the oil sanction would not be nullified by the actions of American oil exporters."[14]

In late November and early December 1935, the question of an oil embargo brought the Italo-Ethiopian crisis to a climax. The United States had indicated cooperation in as positive a manner as it dared, and those who formulated British foreign policy had accepted the likelihood of American support. British public opinion and Mussolini's refusal to compromise except on his own terms were forcing the reluctant British government gradually along the road to further sanctions. The Coordination Committee of the League had scheduled a meeting for November 29 to consider the imposition of the oil sanction, which it had already approved in principle.

Hull's statement of November 15 was an important factor in the decision to call the meeting of the Coordination Committee. Chairman Vasconcellos feared that the American initiative might expose the Committee to charges of vacillation, but he did not want to jeopardize the separate negotiations that Great Britain and France were intermittently carrying on with Mussolini. Consequently, before he called the meeting for November 29, he informally sounded out London and Paris and received their agreement on the date.[15]

The oil sanction now posed an imminent threat to Italy. It

would halt Italy's mechanized army far more effectively than the long-range economic sanctions previously imposed. Aloisi thought Mussolini appeared "extremely nervous on account of the oil sanction." Hull's statement of November 15 and the impassioned criticism of Italian policy he gave Ambassador Rosso on November 22 must have appeared ominous to the Italian dictator. Indeed, three years later, on the eve of the Munich Conference in 1938, Mussolini admitted to Hitler that "if the League of Nations had followed Eden's advice in the Italo-Ethiopian dispute and had extended economic sanctions to oil, I would have had to withdraw from Abyssinia within a week."[16]

Striking the League chain at its weakest link, France, Italian Ambassador Vittorio Cerruti warned French Foreign Minister Laval that Italy would consider an oil embargo as a military sanction. Italy, Cerruti concluded sharply, could not assume the responsibility for the consequences.[17] He did not have to remind France that these might include the renunciation of the Rome Agreements, the collapse of the Stresa front against Germany, and a conflict between Great Britain and Italy. Laval's foreign policy was intended to prevent precisely these possibilities. The French Foreign Minister had aimed at achieving a compromise among his old British friend, his new Italian ally, and—as a distant third—the principles of the League of Nations. "As I have always said," Laval explained to Aloisi, "France cannot break with England. My task remains the same—that of minimizing the measures which the English wish to adopt against Italy while seeking always to satisfy as many as possible of your demands."[18]

With the outbreak of hostilities between Italy and Ethiopia in October 1935, the French left had endorsed the League of Nations and demanded effective sanctions against Italy. "It is by sanctions and not by petty tricks that the Italo-Ethiopian war will be stopped," wrote Socialist leader Léon Blum in his party's newspaper, Le Populaire. He saw no basis at all for a compromise between the League and Italy. On the question of the United States and an oil embargo, Blum and other Socialist leaders had little doubt of American cooperation. "It is certain," Blum argued, "that the United States will take on their part the necessary measures so that the decision of the League of Nations will work fully."[19] Both Le Peuple, official organ of the Confédération Générale du Travail, and the Communist L'Humanité considered the American attitude definitely encouraging and foresaw the imposition of an oil embargo by mid-December.[20]

While the French left insisted on vigorous action to defend the League Covenant, the French right urged compromise and conciliation. The parties of the right, which were inclined to sympathize with Mussolini as a bulwark against Communism and to distrust the League of Nations, insisted on the maintenance of the Italian alliance. They considered the agreement with Mussolini important in the practical sense because it provided additional security against Germany. Moreover, the right feared that the loss of Italian friendship might force France to choose between appeasement of Nazi Germany and reliance on Communist Russia.[21]

The French right strongly opposed an oil embargo because they feared a break with Italy and an upset of the balance of power in Europe. The two most influential conservative newspapers in Paris, Le Figaro and Le Temps, argued repeatedly that the purpose of economic sanctions was "to hasten the re-establishment of peace and not to risk transforming a local conflict into a general crisis."[22] The right realized that the attitude of the United States encouraged the advocates of extended sanctions. "The interpretation which the American government seems more and more disposed to give to the principle of neutrality," Le Temps lamented, "makes quite hazardous the belief in the inefficacy of an oil embargo."[23]

The increasing probability of an oil embargo, which caused Mussolini's threat to break the Franco-Italian alliance, forced the hand of the French government. Premier Flandin and Foreign Minister Laval agreed with the right-wing belief that friendship with Italy superseded the application of the League Covenant. They must have had in mind the warnings of the French Ambassador in Berlin that Hitler had decided to denounce the Locarno Treaty when an appropriate moment occurred.[24] In order to put off the final decision on the imposition of the oil sanction, Laval managed to obtain a postponement of the November 29 meeting of the Coordination Committee on the excuse that urgent parliamentary business required him to remain in Paris. But no one failed to understand this excuse as a mere pretext and to recognize the French inability to face the issue of oil.[25]

The State Department was disturbed by news reports that the postponement of the Committee meeting had disappointed Washington, that the administration was reducing its pressure in regard to Italian trade as a result, and that Hoare had informed the American Chargé in London that the delay would not leave the United States out on a limb.[26] The government had always insisted on the entirely separate and independent nature of American policy. It continually feared that any linking of this policy with Great Britain or the League of Nations might tie the administration's hands in this or any future crisis. A head-on clash with the isolationists could only mean a further limitation on the powers of the President in foreign policy.

Hull insisted vehemently at his press conference on November 26 that American policy had not changed as a result of European events, and that it would not change because the administration intended to follow the letter and spirit of the neutrality law. The government's program, he emphatically asserted, followed first, the desire to keep the United States out of war and as far from hostilities as possible; second, the opposition to war profits and to the United States as a source of war materials; and third, the realization of the complications arising from increased trade between a neutral and a belligerent. Hull had tailored his explanation to fit the notions and prejudices of isolationists, pacifists, and revisionists.

If the United States intended to remain neutral and to keep out of the war, Hull went on to say, the administration could not permit exporters to ship essential war materials abroad for manufacture into military supplies. Continuing in much the same vein he had used with Ambassador Rosso less than a week before, Hull said he did not consider it incumbent on the United States to supply war materials to belligerents to assist them in protracting hostilities, especially in view of the American interest in peace and the United States commitment to the Kellogg-Briand Pact. The government did not intend to permit a few "to gobble up blood profits" by helping belligerents to prosecute a war.

Hull admitted that certain actions taken by the administration appeared similar to those taken by other countries, but he thought these resemblances had been unduly emphasized. He reminded the journalists at his press conference that the United States had not officially designated any nation as an aggressor, nor undertaken to aid one of the belligerents, nor prevented normal trade with belligerents except in armaments. The more one investigated this question, Hull insisted, the more striking the differences were between the American neutrality policy and the policies being applied by foreign peace agencies. Hull said he did not care what people called the neutrality policy because he knew that the administration was carrying out the letter and spirit of the neutrality resolution and at the same time bearing in mind American obligations to the maintenance of peace and the Kellogg-Briand Pact.[27]

The day following Hull's vigorous insistence on the independence of American policy, the State Department checked on press reports that Hoare had assured Chargé Atherton that a delay in oil sanctions would not leave the United States out on a limb. Western European Affairs Chief Dunn read to Atherton a prepared memorandum similar to Hull's explanation to the press and instructed Atherton to issue a denial that Hoare had given him any such "assurance." The State Department felt that the use of that particular word gave the opposition the idea that the United States was working with the League and Great Britain. Atherton insisted that his recent conversations with the Foreign Office had implied nothing of the kind, but Dunn pointed out, nevertheless, that the impression created in the press had worried the Department.[28]

The accuracy of the news reports had forced Hull and Dunn to be emphatic. The implications of the postponement embarrassed the British, who expressed considerable anxiety over the American reaction. The day before Hull's press conference, the Foreign Office had asked Ambassador Bingham to hold himself in readiness for further discussions. On November 28 Hoare explained to Bingham that the government regretted the delay but considered it unavoidable because of the situation in France. On November 30 British Ambassador Lindsay delivered to the State Department an oral communication justifying the postponement: "It would be a calamity," he said, "if responsible people in America were to conclude that the British Government and other members of the League were not prepared to do what they could to restrict oil exports while the American Government was using its moral influence towards bringing about such a restriction."[29]

The American reaction genuinely concerned the British government because an effective oil sanction required some measure of cooperation by the United States. But at the same time Great Britain was not disappointed to see an immediate application delayed, and officials hoped the delay would give them time to reach a compromise solution that would eliminate the need for an oil embargo. The British oral communication suggested that the apparent military stalemate in East Africa and Italy's economic problems might incline Mussolini to compromise. The imposition of an oil embargo, on the other hand, might make Mussolini even more intransigent in an effort to avoid the appearance of being compelled to compromise. The communication concluded that the government would make a serious effort to reach a compromise settlement, and that if negotiations were making progress it might be necessary to postpone the consideration of the oil embargo even beyond December 12.

This oral communication to the State Department definitely indicated that Great Britain was giving serious consideration to some kind of compromise plan. Much to its surprise and annoyance, the British government had found itself driven by public opinion to active support of the League of Nations. The logic of its action had pushed it toward the imposition of an oil embargo. In negotiations with other Mediterranean states, diplomats were securing promises of support if Italy attacked British territories or ships in retaliation.[30] The Cabinet had agreed to impose the oil sanction if necessary and had prepared to say so at the now postponed November 29 meeting, but the postponement came as a great relief.

Caught between its own lack of imagination and the pressure of public opinion, the British government had followed the "double line" of cooperation with the League and separate negotiations with France and Italy. It announced this policy openly, defended it in Parliament, and even argued that the League had approved it.[31] Spokesmen for the government insisted continually that any solution had to have the support of all three parties involved—Ethiopia, Italy, and the League of Nations. What the government really wanted was a compromise settlement that would give victory to neither side, maintain Anglo-Italian friendship, keep Italy in the Stresa front, and save the prestige of the League of Nations. It thus agreed to make one last attempt at compromise before imposing a vital oil sanction. "The change of date," Hoare explained to Parliament on December 5, "means no weakening whatever in the attitude of the member states. It does, however—and this is the point I wish to emphasize this afternoon—give a further opportunity for an intensive effort to bring about a peaceful settlement." Although the atmosphere was tense and it was impossible to reconcile the divergent aims of Italy, Ethiopia, and the League, Hoare nevertheless concluded that "the French and we intend not only to go on trying but to redouble our efforts during the short period of time that is still open before the Geneva meeting."[32]

Mussolini appreciated the opportunity for procrastination presented by this dual policy. The administration also recognized the duality of the British policy and saw no reason to risk a battle in Congress that might well end in the total defeat of its foreign policy and thereby imperil its domestic program. American diplomats had continually reported rumors of double-dealing and intrigue; the postponement of the meeting of the Coordination Committee seemed to substantiate these rumors.[33] Indeed, under the circumstances the administration had taken remarkable initiative in encouraging the League to act positively.

British and French diplomats, led by Maurice Peterson of the Abyssinian Department of the British Foreign Office and Comte de St. Quentin of the African Department of the Quai d'Orsay, had considered compromise solutions continually since the Italian invasion in early October.[34] Two weeks after the invasion Italian Ambassador Cerruti in Paris had given Laval an outline of his country's minimum demands.[35] Mussolini, however, sought far more than the British negotiators could ever concede. The British public viewed the crisis in moral terms; they saw it as brazen aggression by an imperialist power against a defenseless African state in direct violation of the Covenant of the League of Nations and the Kellogg-Briand Pact.

Italians, on the other hand, could not understand why Great Britain, with the world's largest empire, opposed the colonial efforts of Italy. As Anne O'Hare McCormick wrote, "Few among the vocal masses feel any sense of guilt at the aggression in Ethiopia. . . . Many quite honestly sympathize with 'those poor Ethiopians,' bombed and invaded, but only because they have been left so long to fall ill and starve under brutal masters." Italians thought their country was fighting for vital national interests, that sanctions against Italy constituted a grave injustice, and that anyone who opposed the Ethiopian venture had selfish motives.[36] Thus, while British public opinion would concede little if anything as a reward for aggression, Italy demanded what it considered its just rights. The Italians insisted on control in one form or another over the Ethiopian Empire—perhaps by a cession of the non-Amharic areas and a mandate over the remainder.[37] Separated by a moral chasm, Great Britain and Italy had no basis for a compromise settlement.

On December 7, while en route to Switzerland for a vacation, Hoare stopped in Paris at Laval's request to discuss the compromise proposals that Peterson and St. Quentin had drafted. Baldwin and the Cabinet understood that the purpose of Hoare's visit was to reach an agreement with Laval in the hope of resolving the crisis before the imposition of an oil sanction. Hoare had said as much publicly in the House of Commons, but his colleagues did not realize how far he would have to go to get such an agreement.[38]

Laval insisted that an oil embargo would force Mussolini to some desperate action, that France could not agree to such a sanction without making renewed efforts to reach a compromise, and that France had no intention of going to war. Laval did not actually say that France would refuse to aid Great Britain if Italy attacked the British fleet in the Mediterranean, but he did suggest as much to Hoare by pointing out that his country's response would be slow and small. Instead of forcing a showdown with Laval by insisting that France choose between Italy and Great Britain, the unimaginative Hoare let Laval persuade him to agree to an amazing set of proposals.[39]

The Hoare-Laval plan had two chief provisions: (1) for an "exchange of territories" by which Ethiopia would surrender to Italy the Ogaden steppe and a large portion of the highland province of Tigre in return for a seaport on the Red Sea or Indian Ocean; and (2) for a "zone of economic expansion and settlement" for Italy that included virtually all of Ethiopia south of Addis Ababa. This zone would remain a part of Ethiopia but Italy would have exclusive economic rights in it. Hoare and Laval approved the plan in Paris on December 8.

The Anglo-French compromise proposals reached Mussolini in Rome on December 11 and the Ethiopian government in Addis Ababa on the next day. Hoare advised Haile Selassie not to reject the plan, and Laval encouraged Mussolini to make a favorable response. Italy reacted slowly and cautiously. The Italian press indicated that the proposals, though unsatisfactory, did have possibilities, and Mussolini instructed Ambassador Grandi in London to seek clarification.[40]

Mussolini's intentions remain a mystery. The anti-Fascist viewpoint insists that he had decided by December 18 to reject the plan. Mussolini later claimed that he had decided to accept it as a basis for negotiation and that the Fascist Grand Council had prepared to approve it on December 18. Ethiopian expert Guariglia went to bed that evening thinking the crisis was over and woke the next morning to find that Hoare had resigned and Mussolini had withheld approval of the plan.[41] Whatever the exact sequence of events or whatever Mussolini's real view, it is questionable that he would have rejected the plan outright. The cautious but occasionally optimistic tone of the controlled press, Mussolini's tactic in seeking additional explanation about the plan, and his custom of never really committing himself lead to the conclusion that if Great Britain had supported the plan, Mussolini would have accepted it, at least as the basis upon which to negotiate for additional concessions.

Hoare and Laval had just agreed on the final terms of their plan when these terms were leaked to the press on December 9, perhaps by enemies of Laval in the Quai d'Orsay seeking to embarrass him. The two ministers had originally hoped to persuade the belligerents to accept the terms and then to present the agreement to public opinion and to the League of Nations as a *fait accompli*. As a result of the French news leak, however, public opinion in Great Britain raged in indignation at a plan that rewarded the condemned aggressor and did not appear in the least bit warranted by the actual military situation. Prime Minister Baldwin, amazed at the popular uproar, could only assure Parliament cryptically that if the troubles were over, he could present such a strong case for the plan that no member would vote against him.[42] In Geneva, Eden insisted that the plan really contained only proposals for negotiations and that the League would of course have the final say in the matter. On December 18 Baldwin capitulated to the popular clamor, and Hoare resigned as the scapegoat. In a gesture calculated to calm sentiment in favor of the League, Baldwin named Anthony Eden to succeed Hoare as Foreign Secretary. British policy, as Chamberlain maintained on the part of the government, still backed the Covenant, and Great Britain would support the extension of sanctions if everyone else agreed.[43] An oil sanction, however, required British or American leadership, and neither for its own reasons would accept this responsibility.

The Hoare-Laval plan and Hoare's consequent resignation created a sensation in the United States. Senator Vandenberg thought the Franco-British proposals proved that American peace required mandatory neutrality legislation rather than cooperation with the League of Nations. In full agreement with the Michigan isolationist, Senator Borah of Idaho professed to see British chicanery behind the plan and urged that the United States keep out of European embroilments. Hamilton Fish Armstrong, the editor of *Foreign Affairs,* thought "American opinion astounded by Anglo-French abandonment of the League"; he feared that "it ends the public approval of [the] recent tendency to evolve an American policy able to fit in with League policy." An editorial in *Business Week* argued that the Hoare-Laval plan was "one more reason for honest neutrality" and for Roosevelt and Hull to "drop their policy of cooperating with the League's sanctions policy under the pretense of neutrality."[44]

President Roosevelt thought the Anglo-French plan was outrageous. In response to a suggestion by the visiting Archbishop of York that the United States could greatly help in international matters if it belonged to the League of Nations, Roosevelt replied that whatever opinion had developed in America to join, the Hoare-Laval plan had killed it.[45] The London *News-Chronicle* reported a "chorus of condemnation" for the Hoare-Laval plan, especially evident and "nowhere more disastrous" than in the United States. "Americans had come to believe, some of them almost reluctantly," it said, "that the League and its principles were capable of being made effective in the determination of a first-class international dispute. . . . This faith has been for the time at any rate utterly shattered."[46]

Although Germany was neither an oil-producing state nor a

member of the League of Nations, Nazi ambitions were foremost
in the minds of Germany's neighbors and played an important
part in the Italo-Ethiopian dispute. Adolf Hitler's rise to power
in 1933 was a vital factor in Mussolini's timing for the conquest of
Ethiopia. Fear and suspicion of Germany had led Russia, France,
and Great Britain to react, each in its own way, to the conflict in
East Africa. At the same time, however, Germany took an intense
interest in the League's response to Mussolini's defiance and
aggression. The Italian aggression had presented a dilemma to
Hitler: If the League of Nations succeeded in preventing Italian
aggression, the world organization and the principle of collective
security would gain great respect and authority. The success of
the League in this crisis might set an important precedent for the
future when Germany would initiate its own campaign for revision and expansion. On the other hand, an Italian victory over
Ethiopia would gravely weaken both the principle of collective
aid and the powers who might oppose Germany in the future. Yet
there was danger in this, too, because a triumphant Italy might
continue to block German ambitions in Austria and the Balkans
and might even rejoin the Stresa front.[47]

As Italy and the League powers drew farther apart after the
Stresa meeting in April 1935, Mussolini began to cultivate Germany, partly as a warning to Great Britain and France and partly
as an attempt to secure German neutrality. He transferred Ambassador Cerruti from Berlin to Paris during the summer because Hitler and Goering distrusted him. Cerruti's replacement,
Bernardo Attolico, sought immediately to remove the chill that
had set in after the assassination of Austrian Chancellor Dollfuss.[48]

How Germany might profit from the Italo-Ethiopian crisis
would shape the attitude of its government. In the weeks following
the outbreak of hostilities between Italy and Ethiopia in October
1935, Nazi party leaders tended more and more to favor Italy, although German public opinion sympathized with underdog Ethiopia. Watching skeptically as Great Britain gave the impression
of organizing a coalition against Mussolini, the Nazis saw a gradual weakening of both the Stresa front and the Franco-Italian
alliance. To cooperate with Great Britain in sanctions, they felt,
would not secure significant concessions for Germany or lead to
a break between Britain and France. An Italian success, the Nazis

gradually decided, would constitute a better precedent for Germany than a triumphant League.[49]

Although increasingly sympathetic to Italy, German leaders still feared that a compromise settlement of the Ethiopian crisis might bring on an Anglo-Italian *rapprochement* and reunite the League powers against Germany. They also had little faith in Italian military skill. In late 1935 Germany, though benevolently neutral in its uncertainty, apparently preferred prolongation and aggravation of the crisis. Germany therefore maintained a cautious neutrality, refraining from participation in League sanctions but also not expanding greatly its trade with Italy. American Ambassador Dodd suggested that the moral embargo applied by the United States had proved somewhat embarrassing to the Germans: the German government, he said, could not base its neutral attitude on that of the United States because Germany wished to be pro-Italian and the United States did not.[50]

The German capital received the news of the Hoare-Laval plan with consternation but learned of its collapse with great relief. The Anglo-French fiasco must have greatly prejudiced Hitler's views of these two democratic states and caused Mussolini's prestige to soar. Nevertheless, Hitler was far from ready to establish a German-Italian partnership. In the differences between Great Britain and Italy, both guarantors of the Locarno Treaty, Hitler saw his opportunity. The failure of the Anglo-French compromise plan and the continuance of the war in East Africa left Hitler's foes disunited and distrustful and permitted Germany to profit further from the fears and troubles of its neighbors.[51]

Chapter Nine

Neutrality and Oil

The surprise and disappointment that the Hoare-Laval plan aroused among members of the League of Nations eliminated any possibility of imposing an oil sanction in December 1935, when it might have halted the mechanized Italian Army. Instead, the delay not only gave Mussolini additional opportunity to stockpile supplies, but also provided Marshal Badoglio with more time to consolidate the Italian military position in northern Ethiopia for a new and decisive drive southward. Italy had won a reprieve from the oil embargo, but it was beginning to feel the more limited and long-term economic sanctions imposed since November 18. As Mussolini commented, a "speed contest" had begun in which the question was whether Italy could finish the struggle before the next summer's torrential rains and before the long-range economic sanctions upset the Italian economy, or whether the war would drag on over a period of years like so many other colonial wars.[1]

Anthony Eden, who replaced Hoare as Foreign Secretary on December 22,[2] announced that Britain would support a collective oil embargo and that the policy of the government would continue as it had before the Hoare-Laval agreement. Since the consistency and sincerity of British policy before December 1935 were in doubt, Eden's vague reassurances were not very effective. Although Eden himself genuinely supported the League of Nations and its program of sanctions, something was clearly lacking after the collapse of the Hoare-Laval plan: there was no sense of pleasant surprise that the League might prove successful, little enthusiasm among the 50 nations who were tackling for the first time in history an aggressor against international peace and morality, and, most important, no active leadership from a great power such as Great Britain, upon whose initiative League action had been and would have to be based.

In the new year 1936 the focus of attention in the Italo-Ethiopian crisis shifted once again from Europe to America. Great Britain and France had agreed to postpone the November 29 meeting of the Coordination Committee and to renew their efforts toward a compromise—this time because they feared that the United States would cooperate, that an oil sanction would effectively halt Italy, and that Italy would retaliate. The Hoare-Laval proposals had disillusioned supporters of collective security and the League; the failure of the plan had disappointed others; but at the time Europe had no other solution to offer.

Throughout January and February 1936, the League powers stalled, and it became increasingly clear that Great Britain and France did not really want to impose an oil sanction. The inability of the American government to do formally what League states refused to do in any way—limit oil shipments to Italy—was the excuse for inaction. Pierre Laval, in answer to a question about whether France would follow Great Britain in the application of an oil embargo, told the French Chamber of Deputies on December 28 that the United States held the answer. "I cannot," he said, "prejudge the decision which will be taken by Congress, the authority which will or will not be given to Roosevelt, the usage which Roosevelt will or will not make of his powers." The American Congress would consider the question before the meeting of the League Council on January 20, Laval concluded; only then would a decision of whether to put the question before the League be possible.[3]

The Times (London), which in November 1935 had not considered the United States the obstacle to an oil embargo, now argued that the neutrality revision, which Congress would soon discuss, represented a matter of "direct, practical, and immediate concern" to Great Britain: "It must depend largely upon the decisions to be taken by Congress during the next few weeks what, if any, extension of the economic pressure now applied to Italy by the League powers is practicable and desirable."[4]

The American Chargé in Moscow thought the Soviet Union

would take no initiative either in opposing or in supporting an extension of sanctions. Uncertainty about the position of the United States gave Russia an excuse for not taking a definite stand. *Le Journal de Moscou,* the French language organ of the Soviet Foreign Office, stated on January 7 that the question of an oil embargo "reduces itself to establishing whether it is possible to cut Italy off from access to the oil of the United States" and Venezuela.[5] Ambassador Long in Rome noted an abrupt reversal in the views expressed to him by Russian Embassy officials after the Hoare-Laval fiasco. From ardent support of an oil sanction, the Russian Counselor had switched to a desire for settling the conflict as soon as possible, even at the risk of a poor compromise, since only Germany stood to gain from the weakening of Italy.[6]

While the League powers relaxed and awaited the action of nonmember America, Italy paid particularly close attention to what the President would say and what Congress would do. Italy realized that definite American action might compel the reluctant League of Nations to impose an oil sanction. The real question was whether the President could interpret the neutrality legislation to permit cooperation with the League. He enjoyed considerable freedom in determining his own foreign policy, the Paris correspondent of *Il Giornale d'Italia* pointed out: "There are some Americans here in Paris who know him well and who insist that because of his personal sympathy toward Great Britain... President Roosevelt should be able to find a formula capable of satisfying the British Cabinet."[7] *La Tribuna* thought "the decision of the United States" would be of the greatest importance. The United States could not hide behind juridical pretexts or general policy declarations attempting to show the independence of American policy, it insisted, for participation in sanctions in any form would constitute a violation of the spirit of neutrality. The United States "knows perfectly well," *La Tribuna* warned, "that its decision is awaited in Europe as the signal for a new advance in the economic siege of Italy, in the name of the League of Nations and for the exclusive account of a mistaken interest of British imperialism."[8]

The first half of the President's message to Congress on January 3, 1936, dealt with foreign affairs. Roosevelt contrasted the good-neighbor relationships in the Americas with the rest of the world.

The "twin spirits of autocracy and aggression" jeopardize world peace and progress, the President declared. "Nations seeking expansion, seeking the rectification of injustices springing from former wars, or seeking outlets for trade, for population ... fail to demonstrate that patience necessary to attain reasonable and legitimate objectives by peaceful negotiation. ... They have therefore impatiently reverted to the old belief in the law of the sword." Roosevelt understood the perilous trend of events abroad, and he did not keep it a secret from the American people. His message to Congress in January 1936 clearly indicted Mussolini and Fascist Italy.

Roosevelt insisted that the American people "must take cognizance of growing ill will, of marked trends toward aggression, of increasing armaments, of shortened tempers—a situation which has in it many of the elements that lead to the tragedy of general war."[9] But he knew that the power of isolationist sentiment at home prevented him from recommending a positive American policy to oppose this fateful trend. He had to use neutrality legislation indirectly to restrict trade with an aggressor in order not to frustrate the League's economic sanctions. Accordingly, he had announced a twofold neutrality policy to hamper the prosecution of a foreign war by prohibiting the export of arms, ammunition, and implements of war to any belligerent and by discouraging such a nation's use of any American product capable of facilitating the progress of a war.

British officials did not react publicly to the President's message because they had learned long ago not to express anything more than vague opinions about a declaration of American policy. But the British press gave it more coverage than anything from the United States since Roosevelt's message in 1933 disrupting the London Economic Conference.[10] Newspapers interpreted the message to Congress according to their predispositions, as they had in November 1935. Liberal and Labour publications stressed the indictment of dictators and the recommendation of an embargo on raw materials as a definite encouragement to the League. Right-wing papers crowed that the message gave the oil embargo "the coup de grace" and entirely ruled out an extension of sanctions.[11] Government journals were equivocal.

The opposition parties, still bitter over their defeat in the November 14 election because of the government's allegedly dishonest pro-League pretenses, pressed for immediate imposition of an oil sanction. The Labourite *Daily Herald* thought it "fairly sure" that Congress would support the President's request for export restrictions on oil, and it urged League members to stop procrastinating on the issue. The Liberal *News-Chronicle* agreed that American support "should notably ease the vital task of the League in pressing forward with an oil embargo against the Italian aggressor."[12]

Viscount Rothermere's *Evening News* and Lord Beaverbrook's *Evening Standard* hoped that Britain would follow the lead of "peaceful isolation" given by President Roosevelt, "cut away every entanglement which might involve us in other people's wars," and play no part in "any dangerous sanctionist game." The *Daily Mail*, another Rothermere paper, summed up the rightist view by saying that because of the President's message, "NO OIL BAN CAN BE EFFECTIVE."[13] This interpretation horrified the *Daily Herald*, the *Manchester Guardian*, and the *News-Chronicle*, all of which concluded that the right-wing press opposed any oil sanction.[14]

The Times and the *Daily Telegraph* echoed the opposition in welcoming Roosevelt's castigation of autocrats and aggressors, and also added that the new American embargo plan would permit the League greater freedom in applying economic pressure against Italy. *The Times*, however, did not advocate the immediate application of an oil embargo, as the opposition press had; instead it suggested that the sanctions already in operation should not be considered ineffectual.[15]

The views expressed by *The Times* and the *Daily Telegraph* are of interest and importance because of the close association of these newspapers with the Conservative leadership. The government insisted publicly that it still favored an oil sanction if everyone else agreed, but the editorials of its most important journalistic supporters revealed that it would not assert the leadership necessary to impose a new embargo. It had shrunk from such an embargo in November 1935 not because of a belief in the inefficacy of an oil sanction or of a lack of American cooperation but because it feared the Italian reaction. The government also refused to impose an oil sanction early in 1936, arguing this time that the existing sanctions might effectively check Italy—why aggravate the situation and risk war when Mussolini would have to compromise anyway?

The French response to Roosevelt's message and the proposed neutrality bill was similar to the British reaction, and the divergence in attitude of the French press followed the same internal political lines. Nationalist, pro-Italian, right-wing papers, which distrusted the League of Nations and opposed the extension of sanctions to raw materials, feared that the League might take encouragement from Roosevelt's neutrality plan, apply an oil embargo, and thus set off a new and larger war. Conservative newspapers tended to ignore the President's condemnation of Mussolini and to minimize the effect of his neutrality proposals on the Italo-Ethiopian crisis. The pro-government *Le Temps* insisted that Roosevelt's address should not be interpreted as meaning cooperation with the League on an oil embargo, and it warned that "the partisans of this extension will not miss finding arguments in the American message in favor of their thesis." It urged its readers "not to judge the American decision until the texts are definitely voted on and applied by the administration."[16]

The French left, sympathetic to the League of Nations and bitterly hostile to Fascism, welcomed the President's condemnation of autocrats and aggressors and demanded French support for collective security and an oil sanction. The Socialist paper *Le Populaire* attributed to American public opinion the apparent contradiction between the President's "devastating indictment of the powers of fascism and imperialist aggression" and the rather weak embargo proposals. "Europe has deceived and discouraged American goodwill," Léon Blum argued as he blamed Laval and the recent deal with Hoare for dampening American enthusiasm. *L'Humanité* agreed with Blum but concluded that the American attitude would still make an oil sanction effective. The left demanded that Laval stop hiding behind the allegedly uncertain American position and that France join in supporting an oil embargo against Italy.[17]

Alexis Léger, Permanent Secretary General of the Quai d'Orsay, thought the League of Nations would delay the question of an oil sanction pending the results of Congressional debate. Unless the President received discretionary authority in the application of sanctions, he foresaw no extension of trade restrictions to oil. American Ambassador Straus in Paris suggested to Hull that the French and British were preparing to blame the United States for the failure to extend sanctions.[18]

In his message to Congress Roosevelt said, "These words which I have chosen with deliberation will not prove popular in any Nation that chooses to fit this shoe to its foot."[19] Italy could not fail to understand what the President meant and to whom he referred. (Italians even thought that the President's metaphor about the fitting of the shoe was a sly reference to Italian geography.) Italian newspapers did not at first publish the entire text of the address, and in particular, they deleted the strongest and most obvious references to autocratic governments. Although the issue of neutrality was more important in the long run, the criticism of the aggressive and impatient behavior of autocratic regimes especially irritated Italians.

Virginio Gayda, writing in *Il Giornale d'Italia*, labeled the President's message a political speech that sought to bridge the gap between isolationists and internationalists. Gayda rejected "this primitive confusion between the alleged autocracy of Fascism and the desire to threaten peace" and asked sarcastically if Roosevelt considered Russia a democracy, if he could justify conditions in Egypt or India, and if he could explain his own Fascist-like industrial codes. On the question of neutrality, Gayda argued that the "revision proposed by Roosevelt would signify not only an obvious intervention by the United States in the conflict, against any principle of neutrality, but also its adhesion to the League and direct submission to British policy." *La Tribuna* complained that prosperous America simply did not understand the complex problems of Europe: "Incomprehension and oversimplification we can call by the general name of Wilsonianism," and Roosevelt, *La Tribuna* concluded, had fallen into the same trap.[20]

After the enactment of the neutrality resolution in August 1935, the various factions within the American government laid plans for a new and more permanent law to be considered when Congress would reconvene in January. Senator Nye and the pacifist-isolationists drafted a nondiscretionary neutrality bill that would establish a rigid barrier against war, which neither sentiment nor propaganda nor money could overcome. The State Department at the same time began drawing up its own bill, which would give the administration more flexibility in formulating and executing American foreign policy. Secretary Hull reluctantly realized that neither Congress nor public opinion would agree to allow the President to designate any one country as an aggressor, but he did hope that Congress would give the moral embargo legal standing, making it enforceable against increased Italian trade.[21]

The State Department cooperated as much as possible with organizations such as the National Peace Conference, the World Peace Foundation, and the League of Nations Association. Western European Affairs Chief Joseph C. Green suggested that such organizations as these, which advocated cooperation between the United States and other governments for the maintenance of peace, would find themselves in a hopeless position if Senator Nye's policy of mandatory isolation became permanently imbedded in American policy. He recommended an intensive campaign by these organizations in order to influence the Senate.[22]

Since oil was the crux of the problem of cooperation between the United States and the League, the administration's neutrality draft centered on this vital raw material, without which the Italian armies would certainly be stalled. Roosevelt wanted the power to deny belligerents any commodities that had the effect of maintaining or prolonging war.[23] The State Department draft law would give the President this power. Congress, however, would insist that this denial extend to both belligerents, and so the Department was willing to accept an impartial embargo if it covered these important raw materials and if the President received discretion in timing the application. This was unquestionably a retreat by the State Department, but as an election-year compromise, it could be expected to go a long way toward calming isolationist fears and yet retain for the administration some flexibility to cooperate with other governments against an aggressor.[24]

To implement the administration's policy, Congressman McReynolds and Senator Pittman, chairman of the legislative committees on foreign affairs, introduced identical bills on January 3. Under this proposed legislation the President obtained discretionary power to restrict to prewar averages trade in important war materials with both belligerents. Senators Nye and Clark and Representative Maury Maverick of Texas put forward an alternative bill on January 5, following the outline of the administration bill but making the arms embargo automatic at the outbreak of a war and the raw materials clause mandatory. The two neutrality plans had superficial similarities but also an important difference: the administration wanted discretion while the isolationists demanded a fully automatic and mandatory neutrality policy.

Both neutrality bills met strong and immediate opposition in the Senate Foreign Relations Committee. Isolationists opposed the administration's Pittman-McReynolds Bill because they feared, as before, that its discretionary features might lead the United States into foreign entanglements. The isolationists who were inclined toward pacifism, led by Nye and Clark, favored their own bill, which lacked the discretionary provisions of the Pittman-McReynolds proposal. The nationalist-isolationists, led by Borah and Johnson, opposed both neutrality bills as surrendering the freedom of the seas, which they interpreted as America's right to trade freely with anyone anywhere at any time.

American businessmen paid close attention to the problem of neutrality and neutrality legislation because an embargo on foreign trade would directly affect importers and exporters. The neutrality law of 1935 had banned only the export of actual implements of war to belligerents and had scarcely affected American trade. But the administration's effort during late 1935 to discourage commerce with Italy by the moral embargo had aroused considerable opposition among those companies with an established Italian trade. Export-import organizations lobbied cautiously but effectively in early 1936 against neutrality revision and agreed with the nationalist-isolationists that unlimited trade and traditional neutral rights should be maintained. Businessmen with only a small stake in foreign trade could easily suggest sacrificing foreign commerce in order to keep out of war, but importers, exporters, and certain manufacturers could not afford such unselfishness.[25]

Italian-American organizations strongly opposed legislation that might cause discrimination against their mother country and restrict the shipment of raw materials required by Italy in its Ethiopian venture. In contrast with American Negroes, many of whom had taken an early interest in the Fascist threat to Ethiopia, Italian-Americans responded only gradually to the Italo-Ethiopian crisis. But when the full response came, in late 1935 and early 1936, it was far stronger and better organized than that of the more numerous American Negroes.

Italian-American social and cultural organizations and the Italian language press, aided and subsidized by Italy's consular and diplomatic representatives, whipped Italian-Americans into "a state of nationalistic frenzy" during the Italo-Ethiopian crisis. But this nationalism was always more pro-Italian than pro-Fascist. As the years had passed since their emigration from overpopulated and impoverished Italy, Italian-Americans tended to remember only the good things about their country. As one of the more recent immigrant groups in America, they ranked low on the socioeconomic scale, and when Mussolini appeared to be successful in his defiance of Great Britain and the League of Nations, Italian-Americans began to take pride in Italian successes as if they were their own. They did not seem to know or care about Fascism, dictatorship, or war.[26]

Loyal to their mother country, Italian-Americans approved the neutrality resolution of 1935 before its application because there appeared to be no conflict between the United States and Italy. But when the President implemented the resolution upon the outbreak of hostilities in October 1935, Italian-Americans criticized the administration for going beyond the letter of the law in discouraging Americans from trading with belligerents except at their own risk and for exercising the authority specifically granted in the resolution to warn Americans about traveling on belligerent ships except at their own risk. Since these warnings affected only Italy, Italian-Americans thought them discriminatory. *Atlantica* approvingly quoted an October 12 editorial in the *Saturday Evening Post,* which it put forth as representing the consensus of American opinion: "If this country is sensible, it will not only keep absolutely clear of the Italian-Ethiopian embroilment but it will refuse to join any of the world powers in bringing pressure upon either of the parties to it. . . . It is well to be on guard against the forces designed to draw us into the African mess, no matter how indirectly."[27]

The increasing efforts of the administration during October and November to cooperate indirectly with Great Britain and the League of Nations by restricting exports to Italy roused Italian-Americans to direct political action. Hull's statement of November 15 marked the decisive point. Letters and other communications received by both the White House and the State Department prior to November 15 had usually favored the administration's policy, but those received after mid-November ran five to four in opposition, and 90 per cent of the majority were form letters from Italian-Americans. The editor of *Il Progresso Italo-Americano* sponsored a campaign in late November to flood Washington with a million letters. The State Department could obtain no proof of collaboration with the Italian Consulate-General in New York, but it found that local opinion accepted the probability of this connection without question.[28]

The propaganda activity and political effectiveness of Italian-Americans reached a peak during January and February of 1936 as Congress again debated neutrality legislation. Letters and resolutions inundated members of Congress, especially those of Italian-American descent or those from northern districts where Italian-Americans lived and were an important part of the local Democratic organizations. These communications strongly opposed granting the President power to define munitions of war and to determine when to apply the embargo. Congressman Peter A. Cavicchia of Newark, New Jersey, remembered how Roosevelt had applied the discretionary features of the 1935 neutrality legislation. If additional discretionary power were given to him, said Cavicchia, "under the proposed bill, he would surely help England, not Italy." The Italian-American Democrat concluded that "selfishness, greed, and the desire to dominate by brute force must give way to the Golden Rule. I believe this to be to supply all that Italy needs except munitions of war and guns."[29]

Assistant Secretary of State R. Walton Moore complained bitterly about "hyphenated-Italians" and the opposition they had aroused in Congress to the administration's neutrality bill. "You can easily imagine," Moore informed Roosevelt, "how the Italian effort was propagated. I haven't the slightest doubt that the Italian Embassy could give us the whole story." It especially enraged Moore when Italian-American groups admitted that they would support the administration's bill if it would exempt the participants in the Italo-Ethiopian War. Moore thought this the antithesis of neutrality because it would "deliberately . . . increase the overwhelming advantage Italy enjoys."[30]

The Italian Embassy's report for 1936 substantiated Moore's complaint as it described "the brilliant job" accomplished by

Italian-Americans in opposing the administration's neutrality bill. The report boasted that the Italian diplomatic and consular staffs had assisted with all kinds of propaganda—"radio, movies, conferences, letters to newspapers, mass meetings of the numerous Italian community, press contacts, and finally the work of direct persuasion on members of Congress through those of Italian origin and those with Italian constituents or those who have some ideological sympathy for us." Pro-Fascist propaganda, one American analyst concluded, "noticeably influenced the course of American neutrality."[31]

Faced with this diffuse but mounting opposition, the administration retreated. On January 10, with Hull's reluctant approval, the Senate Foreign Relations Committee eliminated from the administration's bill the clause that permitted the President to ban exports whenever he found that the lack of such a restriction "would contribute to a prolongation or expansion of war." The administration's bill still retained a section that authorized a ban whenever the President found it would "serve to promote the security and preserve the neutrality of the United States." Although broad in meaning, the first clause had aroused opposition specifically because Senators Vandenberg, Borah, and others feared it would authorize the President to cooperate with the League of Nations.[32]

The European reaction to the Senate Committee's decision was predictable. In Great Britain the *Daily Mail* rejoiced that the Committee had further "strengthened" the neutrality bill and thus rendered an oil sanction as "dead as the dodo." The *Daily Herald* thought that "attempts being made to fuddle public opinion concerning the meaning of the U.S. Neutrality Bill are really passing all bounds," especially since Hull himself had declared that the change made no practical difference in the President's power to limit oil supplies to peacetime averages. "That was perfectly obvious," stated the *Daily Herald*; "to pretend otherwise is simply ridiculous." The *News-Chronicle* agreed with the *Daily Herald* and urged that the League not concern itself with such "Jesuitical word spinning" and get on with imposing an oil sanction.[33]

The Conservative *Daily Telegraph* continued to equivocate. Without specifically mentioning the United States, on January 20 it declared the time was "not ripe for any decision" on an oil sanction because Italy would still have access to important alternative sources. It suggested that the League Council explore the possibilities of peace because military difficulties in East Africa might have modified the Italian view of acceptable terms. By the end of January the *Daily Telegraph* openly advocated no action on an oil sanction because "the attitude of the United States Congress towards embargoes imposed by the League States upon an aggressor has still to be decided."[34]

The French Socialist paper *Le Populaire* considered the amendment of the proposed neutrality act "a bad omen," though it argued that Roosevelt still had room left for interpretation. But even if the United States did not halt oil shipments to Italy, *Le Populaire* concluded, the small American share of the Italian oil trade could not seriously disrupt a League embargo. The right-wing press, on the other hand, advised delay in the imposition of an oil sanction. The League could not properly decide to embargo oil, *Le Temps* argued, "before the terms of eventual American neutrality are definitely fixed because it is evident that the efficacy of the measure depends in large part on the nature of the cooperation of the United States." Just as in Great Britain, therefore, the anti-Fascist left continued to believe in some form of American participation and to urge immediate imposition of a League oil embargo, while the pro-Italian right called for delay on the grounds that extended sanctions would fail without complete American cooperation.[35]

Il Giornale d'Italia described the Senate amendment in a headline as the "American Blow to the Sanctionist Front" and hopefully interpreted it as proof that "the United States will not join Geneva in imposing the oil sanction." Hull's campaign to persuade the Senate to permit cooperation with the League had failed. *La Tribuna,* suspicious of America after the President's message to Congress, thought that the decision of the Senate Committee began to clarify the situation and to "separate the conduct of the United States from the insane policy of the League."[36]

In the midst of this uncertainty over Congressional action on Roosevelt's embargo plan, the Council of the League met on January 20 and the Committee of Eighteen met two days later.

High League officials admitted that they had arranged these dates in order to let Congress act first on neutrality legislation. They had hoped to use a stronger American embargo to prod the world organization into extending sanctions.[37] But since the United States had not embargoed oil as sanctionists had hoped, those who favored delay kept the upper hand. Increasingly fearful of Germany, cautious League members did not want to risk further League action against Italy. The timid rationalized their inaction by arguing that no action was necessary after all because the Italian armies were stalled in the rugged Ethiopian highlands.[38] And furthermore, they argued complacently, the economic sanctions already imposed upon Italy would soon take effect. Why run the risk of the war continually threatened by Mussolini, they asked, and perhaps throw the Fascist dictator into the arms of his Nazi counterpart by imposing an oil embargo, when the slow process of existing sanctions might effectively halt him?

The Committee of Eighteen, therefore, eliminated from Proposal Four A all raw materials except oil on the grounds of ineffectiveness. But it could not drop oil without admitting publicly that the League had surrendered on the question of an extension of sanctions. The Committee thus used the old delaying device of appointing another committee to examine the feasibility of the question, this time establishing on January 22 a subcommittee of experts.[39]

In Washington, meanwhile, the House Foreign Affairs Committee had approved the administration's bill on January 28, but the crucial struggle took place in the Senate. Conflicting viewpoints in the Senate Foreign Relations Committee during January and early February prevented agreement on any new neutrality legislation. As a result of this impasse, the administration reluctantly concluded early in February that a discretionary bill had little chance and that it would drop the issue until after the November election.[40]

On February 12, with the acquiescence of the administration, the Senate Committee voted unanimously to extend the old neutrality resolution. Indeed, the administration much preferred this solution to any bill that would tie its hands by legislating a rigid procedure and thereby preventing it from any international cooperation to preserve peace. Although strong isolationist sentiment was the basic reason why the administration did not exert more pressure for its flexible neutrality bill,[41] European conditions also dissuaded it from pursuing the issue. American military officials, like those in Europe, thought Italy was in a tight spot in northern Ethiopia. In addition, American diplomats continually advised the State Department that the British government had no interest in an oil embargo.[42]

Although the neutrality resolution of 1936 extended the one of 1935, it included a very important change. The first resolution had not required the President to extend the arms embargo to additional countries that might go to war in defense of the Covenant or the Kellogg-Briand Pact, but the 1936 resolution made this provision mandatory. This only strengthened Anglo-French fears and hesitations.

In signing the neutrality law on February 29, the day the original resolution expired, Roosevelt noted that it included few important commodities necessary for warfare, and he renewed his appeal for voluntary cooperation by American business: "It is true," he said, "that the high moral duty I have urged on our people of restricting their exports of essential war materials to either belligerent to approximately the normal peacetime basis has not been the subject of legislation. Nevertheless, it is clear to me that greatly to exceed that basis, with the result of earning profits not possible during peace, and especially with the result of giving actual assistance to the carrying on of war, would serve to magnify the very evil of war which we seek to prevent."[43]

The subcommittee of oil experts appointed by the Committee of Eighteen to study the effect of an oil embargo submitted its report on February 12, the same day that the Senate Foreign Relations Committee voted to extend the 1935 neutrality resolution. From statements by Committee Chairman Pittman as early as January 29, however, the experts on the League subcommittee had been able to forecast the eventual extension of the old neutrality resolution rather than the adoption of the President's more flexible proposal.

The subcommittee agreed that the Italians would exhaust their oil supply within three and a half months in case of a total prohibition of oil exports to Italy, that the effectiveness of the oil embargo would decrease only slightly if the United States restricted exports to the prewar average, and that even if the United States did not limit exports Italy would find it slow and costly to get the necessary oil. Despite this encouraging report, the spirit of October 1935 had evaporated in the fears that created the Hoare-Laval plan and the suspicions that resulted from it. The Committee of Eighteen merely referred this technical report to member states for political decision and set its next meeting for March 2.[44]

In Great Britain, the Liberal and Labour opposition continued to demand the immediate imposition of an oil embargo and to insist that America was ready to cooperate. Clement Attlee, head of the Parliamentary Labour Party, rejected the idea that the attitude of the United States accounted for the delay in imposing an oil restriction. The real cause of the delay, he said, "was the reluctance of the two leading States in the League to impose oil sanctions because they had been following a policy of alliances at Stresa." The American government and people, Attlee insisted, had prepared to collaborate with the League in November: "It may be much more difficult now, but I think it is possible." Even if the Hoare-Laval plan had shocked Americans, he concluded, "is it any reason why the rest of the League should not put on oil sanctions?"[45]

The right wing *Daily Mail* proclaimed self-righteously that "the fanatical devotees of the League . . . might have known from the first what would happen. There was never the remotest chance," it said, of American cooperation. The experts agreed, according to the *Daily Mail,* that the embargo would not work without the support of the United States, and the newspaper rejoiced that the Senate had taken special care to prevent such support by killing the bill. The right wing urged Britain to follow the American example and mind its own business.[46]

The speeches of Cabinet members in the House of Commons and the editorial opinions of pro-government newspapers made it clear that the British government did not favor an oil embargo and was looking for a scapegoat. Foreign Secretary Anthony Eden took care never to mention the United States by name. But in the House of Commons on February 24, he argued that the League aimed at the "cessation of hostilities," that an oil embargo had to be judged on the basis of its probable effectiveness in halting the war, and that oil was "a commodity the supply of which was largely in the hands of a nonmember of the League." Eden's conclusion was unmistakable: American failure to guarantee cooperation had prevented the imposition of an oil sanction.[47]

The Times and the Daily Telegraph emphasized what Eden implied. They agreed that an oil sanction could have been imposed if the President's proposed neutrality bill had passed. But without American legislation, they concluded, an oil sanction would mean little; moral suasion had not worked. The Daily Telegraph declared emphatically that "the decision of the League depended on the decision of Washington!" The Times described the important Italian military breakthrough at Amba Alagi in February 1936 as only "the beginning of a long and costly series of operations" and repeated the refrain that the war effort had seriously drained Italian resources. "There does not seem much for the League Powers to do," declared The Times, "except to maintain their collective resistance to aggression and their common front, each Power keeping in step with all the others, neither lagging behind nor pressing forward in isolated action." Great Britain could not have made it any clearer that it was refusing to take further action.[48]

French Socialists and Communists complained bitterly that the "hesitations of the League" and the "intrigues of Laval" had pushed the United States into isolation. Both Le Populaire and L'Humanité pointed out, nevertheless, that the oil experts considered an oil sanction of considerable effect even without American participation. Positive action by the League would certainly influence the United States, they urged, and in any case, League members could greatly restrict the transportation of American oil to Italy because they controlled the bulk of the world's tanker fleet.[49] The French right, on the other hand, emphatically opposed an oil sanction. Le Temps noted "that the United States, without which economic sanctions are ineffective, has backed out." Somewhat disingenuously because of its lack of sympathy for the League in the past, it argued that stricter but ineffective sanctions would strike a serious blow at the League's authority and prestige. Le Temps also expressed hope that recent Italian victories might have assuaged Italian honor and made Italy more disposed to compromise along the lines of the Hoare-Laval plan.[50]

The action of the American Senate in extending the 1935 neutrality resolution proved vitally important to Italy. Approval of the President's flexible neutrality proposal would almost certainly have forced the reluctant hand of the League into imposing an oil embargo. Italian newspapers rejoiced that "the question of American neutrality is closed with the defeat of the American collaborationists and the European Leaguers." To *Giornale* editor Gayda, this seemed confirmation of his hope that Americans would concern themselves with the problems of the Western Hemisphere and stay out of Europe's affairs. Mussolini himself took notice in a speech to the Council of Ministers on March 3, three days after Roosevelt had signed the extension of the neutrality resolution. Congress, said Mussolini, had "rejected every proposal to extend the list of commodities now under embargo and paid not the slightest attention to the solicitations of the League. As Italians we cannot fail to receive with satisfaction this direction of American policy, but I desire to add that the American Congressmen and Senators who refused any embargo on oil and other raw materials have rendered above all a precious service to the cause of world peace."[51]

Italy, delighted that the United States had refused to assume the initiative necessary to spur the frightened and complacent League powers into imposing an oil sanction, knew very well the sympathies of Roosevelt and his administration. The annual report of the Italian Embassy in Washington for 1936 summarized the President's foreign policy as one of economic collaboration and political neutrality "not free from a strong preferential sympathy for countries with democratic regimes." The Embassy thought Roosevelt had become confused and uncertain after his failure to achieve cooperation with the democratic states "in the attempt to obtain from Congress the approval of a neutrality law which would have exercised pressure on Italy during the Ethiopian conflict." The American people, concluded the Italian Embassy, considered Italy a violator of the Kellogg-Briand Pact, an aggressor against a defenseless people, and the nation that was responsible for "the failure of the policy of collective security, a policy to which the United States, even if it intends not to make any active contribution, remains for ideological reasons profoundly attached."[52]

Chapter Ten

Victory and Defeat

When the members of the Committee of Eighteen arrived in Geneva on March 2 to discuss the views of other League members on the report of the oil experts, none seriously thought that the imposition of an oil sanction would be possible. The United States government, by its inability to secure neutrality revision, had indicated that it could not take the initiative, and Great Britain had allowed matters to drift since the Hoare-Laval agreement of the preceding December. The fact that only Great Britain brought its oil expert to Geneva illustrated the lack of confidence other members of the Committee felt in the continuous British protestations of support for a collective oil embargo.[1] Anthony Eden's inactivity as Foreign Secretary, moreover, hardly encouraged those who hoped that enlightened leadership might establish the League of Nations as a powerful agency for peace.

The threat of an oil sanction in March 1936 seemed far less imminent and serious to Italy than it had in November 1935. Italy had accumulated stockpiles of raw materials, and the once-stalled Italian armies had begun an important offensive in northern Ethiopia. Mussolini, however, thought the threat serious enough to justify applying the same kind of pressure on the new French Foreign Minister, Pierre Flandin, that he had applied earlier on Pierre Laval. On instructions from Rome, Renato Bova Scoppa, Secretary of the Italian Delegation at Geneva, warned Flandin that if the League embargoed oil, Italy would abandon it, denounce the Rome Agreements, and perhaps even ignore the Treaty of Locarno.[2] The Italian press emphasized Mussolini's warning by magnifying rumors of an Italian-German agreement.

As soon as the Committee of Eighteen met on March 2, Flandin asked for a postponement of consideration of the oil report until the Council could make a fresh attempt to seek conciliation and an end to the hostilities. Eden, under instructions to take no initiative,[3] immediately agreed with Flandin but then informed the surprised Committee that Great Britain would join in an early application of an oil sanction if other League members would do likewise. He did not refer to the incomplete League membership or important nonmembers, the usual British excuse for inaction.[4]

Eden took his strong stand for the record only, making it as he did after his concurrence in Flandin's plea for postponement. British public opinion had grown anxious over Italian victories in Ethiopia and outraged over Italy's use of poison gas and its bombing of clearly marked Red Cross missions. The opposition was savagely attacking the government for lack of effective leadership and positive action, and Eden obviously intended his Geneva statement for domestic political consumption.[5]

The Council's Committee of Thirteen, which comprised the regular members except Italy (since no nation involved in a dispute could vote) met on the following day, March 3. It unanimously approved Flandin's resolution to appeal to Italy and Ethiopia "for the immediate opening of negotiations in the framework of the League of Nations and the spirit of the Covenant with the view to a prompt cessation of hostilities and a definitive restoration of peace." The Committee agreed to meet again on March 10 to "take cognizance" of the replies. Haile Selassie accepted on March 5, although it was reported that Ethiopians distrusted the term "conciliation" because they thought it meant they would have to make heavy material concessions while the aggressor would be asked only to sacrifice part of his unrealized hopes.[6] Three days later Mussolini also acquiesced, but without reference to the framework of the League or the spirit of the Covenant.

Mussolini had accepted the invitation to negotiate with Ethiopia after the sudden German occupation of the Rhineland on March 7, 1936. He certainly would have agreed anyway, at least to have a talking point and a delaying tactic, but now he saw another opportunity to use to his advantage the Anglo-French fear of Nazi Germany. (Hitler had decided to invade the Rhineland some time before and had bided his time while the League was proving itself incompetent to handle Italy. The French ratification of the Franco-Soviet Pact on February 27 had given him the excuse he wanted, and the bitter division among his potential foes over the Italo-Ethiopian crisis had made him confident in his plan.)[7]

During March 1936 as the attention of the world was focused on Germany and the Rhineland, Italian armies pressed rapidly southward on the road to Addis Ababa. France and Great Britain reversed positions, the French pleading for joint action against Germany and the British seeing new hope in Hitler's promises for peace. The British argued that Germany had not started a war or crossed national boundaries; Hitler, they said, had merely sent troops into the Rhineland, Germany's backyard. The French pointed out that Ethiopia was in Africa but the Rhineland was in Europe, and on French borders at that. On March 19, Eden, Flandin, and the Italian and Belgian representatives presented a draft resolution to the Council insisting that all parties concerned with the Rhineland dispute show scrupulous respect for treaty obligations!

On March 23 the Council returned briefly to the Italo-Ethiopian dispute. Mussolini had used every technique of delay and ambiguity to parry League efforts while his armies struck southward. Italy was using airplanes and poison gas in a race to seize Addis Ababa before the torrential summer rains began. Mussolini scarcely hid his contempt for the League, but he did not withdraw, because he feared losing his bargaining position. The decisive military encounter took place at Lake Ashangi in northern Ethiopia between March 31 and April 3. Haile Selassie took personal command and in hopeless heroism flung his last organized army at Italy. The Italians decimated the Ethiopians, the Emperor escaped in disguise on a donkey, and the road to Addis Ababa lay open.

The British government gradually realized in April that Italy had won, that the gamble of limited sanctions had failed, and that Britain would have to make the best of the matter, however distasteful and bad for British prestige that would be. At the same time the government could not openly admit to this position. It would have to pretend to support the League and an oil sanction until it could persuade British public opinion that it had exerted all the leadership and taken all the action it reasonably could.[8] Eden admitted to Aloisi on April 20 that he really did not support sanctions: "I am forced to speak in this way," he said. Aloisi answered that Eden was "a prisoner of a parliamentary situation" that he had created for himself.[9]

Previously Geneva had considered increasing the severity of sanctions, but the current had obviously changed. The British now had to maneuver carefully to maintain even the existing program of limited restrictions on Italy. Eden admitted that the collective effort against Italy was "slipping badly. We have done our best," he said, "but I fear it is going to crumble."[10] Britain now hoped, but did not expect, that Haile Selassie could hold on until the coming of the summer rains, which would stall Mussolini as effectively as an extension of sanctions.

The British opposition castigated the lack of initiative and leadership in the Conservative government. Labour leader Clement Attlee asked what the government had done in the five months since the League had agreed in principle on an oil sanction. Liberal leader Archibald Sinclair complained that it was "not the policy of sanctions which failed; it is the resolution of the Government which has failed." When a member interrupted, "You mean war?," Sinclair answered immediately that he meant "assistance to the victim of aggression and if, while we are giving that assistance to the victim, the aggressor attacks us, certainly we must firmly resist."[11]

Eden insisted that Great Britain had taken the initiative in keeping the crisis before the League and had failed because the sanctions had not taken immediate effect; an oil embargo, he said, would have had slight value without universal League membership.[12] Prime Minister Baldwin rationalized that the League was bound to be ineffective without the membership of such major powers as the United States, Germany, and Japan.[13] Other Conservatives, disregarded diplomatic niceties and directly accused the United States of making an oil embargo ineffective: "What is the value of urging His Majesty's Government to insist on the imposition of an embargo on the export of oil to Italy," one Conservative asked on April 9, "if, in fact, that embargo must be ineffective . . . on account of the situation of the United States."[14]

The question of American cooperation in an oil embargo constantly came up in Parliament's debates and question periods on foreign policy. On May 6 Sinclair said it was quite clear that if the "oil sanction had been imposed when it was first adopted in principle by the Committee of 18 in Geneva, it would have received warm support in the United States of America." But Undersecretary Cranborne opposed this view. If it was the Hoare-Laval plan that had destroyed American willingness to help, he asked, why was it that American oil exports to Italy soared in the months before the plan, when the American people were said to have sympathized so deeply with the Ethiopians? "All our evidence shows," he went on, "that there was, at no time, a great probability of the United States cooperating." If an oil sanction had been applied, he concluded, "it would have had to be put on by the League without the assistance of the United States."[15]

The British government continually boasted that it had taken the lead at Geneva. But whenever an opposition member of Parliament asked what it was going to do about stopping Italy, the government always answered that the League would make the decision and that Britain would do its part in collective enforcement. For example, Seymour Cocks asked Eden on April 27 if he would propose joint action by the League powers to prevent passage of supplies of poison gas through the Suez Canal. Eden replied ambiguously that "the steps which are to be taken by the League with regard to the Italo-Abyssinian dispute will be the subject of joint consideration by the States concerned during the forthcoming meeting of the Council on 11th May." Cocks repeated his original question, "Do the Government propose to raise the question of poison gas passing through the Suez Canal?" When Eden gave no reply, Cocks demanded, "Will the right hon. Gentleman answer the question on the paper?" Eden responded weakly, "I think it will be recognized that I have answered the question." Cocks did not think so; he repeated his question: "I asked whether the Government propose to put the proposition before the League at their next meeting." Eden peremptorily concluded the exchange by stating flatly that "pending deliberations at Geneva," he was not prepared to make any statement.[16]

The failure of the League to impose an oil embargo or to close the Suez Canal gave Mussolini sufficient time to achieve a military victory before the summer rains and the existing sanctions would have forced him to compromise. Under the leadership of

Marshal Badoglio, who had replaced General de Bono in November 1935, the Italian armies consolidated and regrouped for a drive on Addis Ababa. Aided by large-scale use of mustard gas and the failure of the Ethiopians to employ the guerrilla tactics so well suited to their situation and geography, the Italians broke Ethiopian military resistance in early April and captured Addis Ababa a month later. Haile Selassie escaped on a British warship to Palestine and then to a lonely five-year exile in England. Although most of Ethiopia was not under effective Italian control, Mussolini declared Ethiopia irrevocably Italian and boasted that after fifteen centuries the Roman Empire had reappeared.[17]

Mussolini assured Ward Price, the correspondent of the sympathetic British *Daily Mail,* that Italy had become a "conservative" and "satisfied" power, with no further colonial ambitions, and would extend the hand of friendship to Great Britain.[18] But he was conciliatory in words only, as he had been throughout the Italo-Ethiopian crisis. His annexation of all of Ethiopia and his proclamation of a new Roman Empire—gestures that would make it difficult for Britain and the League to accept his victory—revealed his contempt for the democracies and the League of Nations.

The sanctionist states found it difficult enough to admit defeat. The halfway measures of the British government had failed, and it would have to continue to temporize until public opinion agreed on lifting sanctions and resuming normal relations with Italy. The opposition, acting as it had throughout the crisis, demanded not only the maintenance of existing sanctions but the inclusion of oil. Conservatives, however, had generally stopped short of measures that might lead to war. Because existing sanctions had failed to halt Italy and because an oil embargo, they thought, would bring war, Conservatives gradually stopped supporting the sanctions already in effect. The government had to mark time during the spring of 1936 while British anger and frustration subsided.

On June 10 Neville Chamberlain, Chancellor of the Exchequer, clearly indicated the approaching end of sanctions against Italy when he described the pressure of Britain's League of Nations Union for the maintenance and even the intensification of punitive restrictions as "the very midsummer of madness" involving "a risk of war." The wavering government needed a lead, Chamberlain thought, and he admitted that he had not consulted Eden, who "would have been bound to beg me not to say what I proposed." The next day in Parliament Prime Minister Baldwin parried and then refused to respond to Attlee's demand for a yes or no answer as to whether Chamberlain's speech represented the government's policy. Baldwin admitted that it raised a number of interesting questions worthy of consideration but that no conclusions had yet been reached.[19]

Eden's address to the House of Commons on June 18 provided the answers. In the past the government had countered opposition questions by insisting on collective responsibility and asserting Britain's willingness to do its share. But now Eden solemnly announced that the British government had a responsibility to the League, "a responsibility not only for compliance, but also for guidance." The government could easily say that it would "act fully and loyally in line with any action which the Assembly of fifty nations may decide upon," he observed, but such a statement "would not be heroic or responsible in a period of difficulty in the League's history." Great Britain, therefore, would aid the League in its perplexity and assume leadership by recommending the lifting of sanctions against Italy. As a reason for the failure of the government and the League, Eden pointed to what he called the serious miscalculation by military opinion that the conflict would last long enough for sanctions on raw materials controlled by the League members to become effective. Without mentioning the United States by name, Eden concluded that the League could not have imposed further sanctions because of its incomplete membership; a sanction on oil "could not be made effective by League action alone."[20]

The session of the League Assembly that began on June 30 was gloomy. The Assembly's resolution of July 4, in addition to reluctantly recommending the raising of sanctions, noted that "various circumstances have prevented the full application of the Covenant of the League of Nations."[21] It tactfully did not specify these various circumstances. Following this recommendation by the Assembly, the Coordination Committee voted to raise the sanctions on July 15.

With the extension of the American neutrality resolution in late February, the refusal of the League to impose an oil embargo in early March, and the increasingly successful Italian military action in March and early April, the role of the United States in the Italo-Ethiopian crisis all but ceased. To the very end the administration continued to discourage trade with belligerents, but it made no new efforts to assume an internationalist position.[22]

The 1936 Report of the Italian Embassy in Washington noted that "the atmosphere of hostility and of uncomprehension" toward Italy was even greater in 1936 after "the vote on the neutrality law put the United States out of the danger of being drawn into the ranks of the sanctionists." Some of the more outspoken anti-Italian newspapers even suggested, the report continued, that it was poison gas that was responsible for the success of the Italian troops. In this attitude toward Italy and in the suspicions about Great Britain, American public opinion found "reasons for reinforcing its own isolationism."[23]

Just before Haile Selassie fled his capital on May 2, 1936, to exile in England, he received Cornelius Van H. Engert's credentials as American Minister to Ethiopia. "Considering the tragic hour in his country's history," Engert wrote to Hull, "he showed remarkable sangfroid and conducted the interview with the same gracious unhurried suavity which had always impressed me on previous occasions. His frail body seemed perhaps a trifle frailer and his thoughtful deepset eyes showed a profoundly perturbed soul. But his handshake had its usual firmness and his inscrutable features were lit up by the same winsome smile." After receiving Engert's credentials, Haile Selassie referred to the President's vigorous denunciation of dictatorships. "The Emperor held my hand in his," wrote Engert, "while he said, 'Convey my greetings to your President and tell him the fate of my country may serve as a warning that words are of no avail against a determined aggressor who will tear up any peace pacts whose terms no longer serve his purpose.' "[24]

After the Emperor's escape and the Italian occupation of Addis Ababa, the State Department began to consider revocation of the President's proclamations. The neutrality resolution provided that "when in the judgment of the President the conditions which have caused him to issue his proclamation have ceased to exist he shall revoke the same." On May 9, four days after the Italian entry into the Ethiopian capital, Hull asked Engert's opinion about whether the war had definitely ended. The American policy on revocation of the proclamations would proceed independently of the decisions of other countries, Hull insisted, and would follow "the facts of the situation" with no relation whatsoever to any question of the recognition of sovereign rights over the territory. Hull wanted to know whether all effective resistance had ceased and if any executive authority other than the Italian occupation forces existed.[25]

Chargé Kirk from Rome and Minister Engert from Addis Ababa kept the State Department informed. Engert pointed out that large areas, especially those south of the Blue Nile and west of Addis Ababa, had escaped Italian control, that Italian convoys faced regular attacks, and that military rule was still the fact. From what Kirk learned from Italian sources of information in Rome, he concluded in mid-June that the Italians had established an executive authority and that effective military resistance no longer existed. On June 12 Hull advised Roosevelt that the government take no action pending further clarification of the situation.[26]

In a more detailed report on June 18 Engert noted that Italy did not even nominally control 40 per cent of Ethiopia and that Italian military columns of less than 1,000 dared not move more than five miles from the capital. The Italians themselves, Engert added, admitted grave anxiety over their small garrison in Addis Ababa, fearing that the approaching rains would severely hamper them.

Engert suggested that revocation of the neutrality proclamations would "assume a very definite political and diplomatic significance which the Department would presumably wish to avoid" since "the Italian Government would at once seize upon it as an indication that America desires to give a lead in an attack upon the sanctionist front." The Italian press demonstrated that Engert's fear was well-founded by continually publishing optimistic reports on the imminent revocation of the American embargo. Engert concluded that all indications were that the Italian treatment of foreigners in Ethiopia was very high-handed. He urged that the State Department, therefore, might "very properly evince concern regarding the future treatment of American interests at the hands of the Italians before taking a step which cannot but be exceedingly pleasing to the Italian Government."[27]

But on June 20 President Roosevelt revoked his proclamations of October 5, 1935, and of February 29, 1936. Hull's recommendation for revocation of the embargo, made on the previous day, insisted that American policy continue to be independent. Hull buttressed his advice with references to international law to the effect that the established government of Ethiopia had collapsed and its military remnants were merely following guerrilla tactics.[28]

What had happened since June 12, when Hull had advised, and Roosevelt had apparently agreed, that no action be taken on the proclamations? Although Hull might have wanted American policy to appear independent and the selections from international law might have seemed appropriate, certainly the most important "fact of the situation" was the British attitude. Chamberlain's statement of June 10 that the continuance of sanctions would be "the very midsummer of madness" indicated a shift in British thinking. Eden's frank statement to the House of Commons on June 18 that Britain would propose the raising of sanctions made British policy clear and indicated the probable action of the League. The administration, therefore, hastened to revoke its neutrality proclamations. This timing offered the advantage of allowing action before the League made its decision but without embarrassing either Britain or the League.

British Conservatives used Roosevelt's revocation proclamation as evidence for the end of the Italo-Ethiopian War and as an additional argument for the raising of League sanctions. Home Secretary John Simon thought no one would suggest that anything the British government had done had caused the President's action; he told the House of Commons that Roosevelt "did it because the war had come to an end."[29]

The United States, which had sought to encourage and cooperate with Great Britain during the Italo-Ethiopian conflict, had again accepted the British lead by revoking its arms embargo. Great Britain, which had not wished to follow an active policy in the dispute, had again used an American action to justify one of its own. The lack of leadership by great powers had ended in the victory of Fascist Italy and the defeat of the League of Nations.

Chapter Eleven

Conclusion

The revocation of the American neutrality proclamations on June 20, 1936, and the lifting of the League of Nations program of economic sanctions on July 15 marked the official end of the Italo-Ethiopian crisis. The diplomatic conflict lingered on, however, for ticklish questions remained, such as the status of Ethiopian delegates at Geneva, the recognition of the Italian conquest, and the accreditation of diplomatic representatives. The British and American public did not forget the Italo-Ethiopian War, and the Italian defiance of international law in the crisis had greatly affected their view of Mussolini, Fascism, and Italy. But in the summer of 1936, the victory of Fascist Italy and the defeat of the League of Nations had to be faced, even if reluctantly.

In December 1936 Great Britain and France, hoping to eliminate the Ethiopian conflict as a cause of friction between themselves and Italy and thus to reestablish the Stresa front against Germany, replaced their legations in Addis Ababa with consulates-general, a move that meant *de facto* recognition. Although Italy very much desired such international acquiescence and recognition, Mussolini never encouraged a *rapprochement* with Great Britain and France by anything more than words. Moreover, his flagrant intervention in the Spanish Civil War in July 1936 and the declaration of the Rome-Berlin Axis in October of the same year indicated the continuing trend in Fascist foreign policy.

Although the United States, like Great Britain, hoped to pre-

vent Hitler and Mussolini from joining hands, it never recognized
in any way the Italian conquest and annexation of Ethiopia. (The
Soviet Union was the only other major government to follow this
course.) Unlike Great Britain and France, the United States did
not play a direct role in European diplomacy and had no interests
in Ethiopia comparable to the French investment in the railroad
to Addis Ababa and the British concern about Lake Tana and the
Blue Nile. More important, the United States would have found
it extremely difficult to recognize the brazen Italian aggression and
total occupation of Ethiopia without also recognizing the Japanese
puppet regime in Manchuria.

The problem of official recognition of Italy's conquest arose
almost immediately after the Italo-Ethiopian War ended. Both
American Ambassador Long in Rome and Italian Ambassador
Rosso in Washington had completed tours of duty in the summer
of 1936. The State Department gave the new American envoy,
William Phillips, credentials accrediting him, as it had accredited
former ambassadors, to the "King of Italy." The new Italian representative, Fulvio Suvich, on the other hand, carried credentials
from the "King of Italy and Emperor of Ethiopia." The United
States would not accept Suvich until Italy agreed not only to receive Phillips but also to understand that its *agrément* in regard
to Suvich would not signify American recognition of the act of annexation.[1] The American government's decision not to demand
a change in Suvich's credentials was attributed by Suvich "to the
interested intervention of Phillips, who wished to be sent to
Rome." Suvich also explained that Mussolini did not refuse to receive Phillips because of "the conciliatory attitude of the Royal
Government, which desired to discriminate in favor of America,
a country which despite all had not joined in sanctions."[2] The
United States had not taken as firm a stand as it had in Manchuria,
but it did not back away from its advanced position.

In June 1936 the State Department terminated the Italian-
American Treaty of Commerce and Navigation of 1871. The Italo-
Ethiopian War had shown that such treaties guaranteeing freedom
of trade might conflict with neutrality legislation. In addition, the
State Department had long felt that this particular treaty was in
practice discriminatory to the United States since Italy's increasingly restrictive quotas, import licenses, and exchange controls had

not existed in 1871. While the United States was limited by Italy's new trade regulations, the treaty required it to afford Italy the benefits of the American reciprocal trade program. The United States might have abrogated the treaty in any case, but its doing so in June 1936 carried definite overtones of condemnation of the recent Italian aggression. These overtones became more positive when the American government refused to agree to a new treaty so long as Mussolini insisted that its preamble recognize the King of Italy as Emperor of Ethiopia.

Before the Italo-Ethiopian crisis, the United States had considered Mussolini not so much a dictator as a strong leader seeking to bring order and prosperity to an impoverished country. After 1935, however, Mussolini appeared to Americans not only as an autocrat but as one who had planned and perpetrated overt aggression. The American people had seen the supposedly civilized and cultured Italians throw poison gas on the allegedly primitive and barbarous Ethiopians. As Ambassador Phillips explained, the "American Government and people had not forgiven Italy for its ruthless campaign against Ethiopia."[3]

The pace of events in Europe quickened after the Italian triumph over Ethiopia and the League of Nations. The Spanish Civil War broke out in July 1936, and Mussolini and Hitler supplied Franco with men and equipment to overthrow the Republican government. In October 1936 Italy and Germany joined in the formation of the Rome-Berlin Axis, and a year later Italy withdrew from the League of Nations. In March 1938 Mussolini acquiesced in the German seizure of Austria and later in the year supported Nazi designs on Czechoslovakia at the Munich conference. A year later, in September 1939, German troops invaded Poland, and Britain and France went to war.

It became increasingly obvious that Mussolini was playing the junior role in the totalitarian alliance and that the Anglo-French policy of indecision and compromise during the Italo-Ethiopian crisis had led to both the collapse of the League of Nations and the disruption of the united front against Germany. In the United States, the worse the European situation appeared, the more determined American public opinion became to stay out of it.

President Roosevelt hoped that Mussolini might be brought to reason in the late 1930's and made several overtures to him. Mussolini, however, was a captive of the trend of events that he himself had helped set in motion by seeking imperial glory in Ethiopia. For example, early in 1939 several American diplomats in European capitals suggested that the President attempt another personal appeal to Mussolini. On March 22, 1939, Roosevelt received the new Italian Ambassador, Prince Colonna, and surprised him with the advice that Mussolini had an excellent opportunity to avert a European conflagration and probably secure desired concessions from a grateful Europe. Mussolini replied two weeks later with the long-planned subjugation of tiny Albania.[4]

On April 15, 1939, the President asked the leaders of Italy and Germany to demonstrate the sincerity of their constantly reiterated peaceful sentiments by giving assurances that they would not attack 31 specified European and Near Eastern nations. Five days later Mussolini described Roosevelt's suggestion as "absurd," a "Messiah-like message" coming from a "distant spectator."[5]

The suspicions engendered on both sides by the Italo-Ethiopian crisis had made it difficult to reestablish the amity that had existed between the United States and Italy before 1935. However much Italians might speak of their gratitude for the American refusal to revise the neutrality law, they realized that Roosevelt and Hull had wanted to cooperate with the League of Nations and to indicate that the United States would not permit American exporters to make an oil sanction ineffective. Moreover, the continued refusal of the United States to recognize the Italian conquest of Ethiopia irritated Italians. Though Roosevelt agreed to make several overtures to prevent a European war, he considered Mussolini a "madman" and the Fascists a pack of "gangsters."[6]

On June 10, 1940, at Charlottesville, Virginia, Roosevelt addressed the graduating class of the University of Virginia. After summarizing his personal attempts to persuade Mussolini not to go to war, he stated indignantly that the Italian government had shown "its unwillingness to find the means through pacific negotiations for the satisfaction of what it believes are its legitimate aspirations. On this tenth day of June, 1940," he said, "the hand that held the dagger has struck it into the back of its neighbor." Fascist Italy had joined Nazi Germany in the Second World War. The President concluded his vigorous address with a historic promise and a determined call to action: "We will extend to the opponents of force the natural resources of this nation, and at the same time we will harness and speed up the use of those resources in order that we ourselves in the Americas may have equipment and training equal to the task of any emergency and every defense."[7] President Roosevelt's speech was the culmination of events and feelings that had begun with the Italo-Ethiopian crisis.

* * *

The Italo-Ethiopian crisis had set the stage and arranged the characters for the Second World War. Great Britain and France, hovering between support of the League of Nations in order to restrain aggressors and friendship for Italy in order to maintain the coalition against Germany, had failed to halt the Italian occupation of Ethiopia but had antagonized Mussolini enough to lead Italy into a German alliance. The United States government, which could not participate directly in League policies against Italy because of isolationism at home, had nevertheless sought to indicate clearly to Britain and France that it would find means not to sabotage effective League action, particularly the proposed, but never implemented, oil sanction. Overwhelmed by the fear of Germany, British and French leaders had temporized and sought compromise —until Mussolini's troops had made the question academic by occupying the Ethiopian capital in May 1936. Despite the fact that American public opinion had condemned the Italian aggression against Ethiopia, no corresponding shift away from the dominant isolationist belief developed. Indeed, the failure of Britain, France, and the League to block Italy only served to widen the tragic gap between Roosevelt's and Hull's growing awareness of America's international responsibilities and the determination of the American public to avoid European entanglements.

Notes

Notes

Chapter One

1. *New York Times,* October 4, 1935, by Pittman B. Potter, an American citizen and international lawyer who represented Ethiopia in arbitrating the Wal-Wal dispute.

2. I am greatly indebted for the general background and development of the Italo-Ethiopian crisis to Arnold J. Toynbee, *Abyssinia and Italy* (London, 1936), and Francis P. Walters, *A History of the League of Nations* (London, 1952), Vol. II.

3. Maurice Vaussard, *De Pétrarque à Mussolini: évolution du sentiment nationaliste italien* (Paris, 1961), pp. 247 and 255.

4. *Ibid.,* Chapt. 15, "La période ascendante de l'impérialisme fasciste," pp. 255–63.

5. Dante L. Germino, *The Italian Fascist Party in Power: A Study in Totalitarian Rule* (Minneapolis, 1959), pp. 11 and 23.

6. Paolo Monelli, *Mussolini: The Intimate Life of a Demagogue* (New York, 1954), pp. 20 and 136. The original Italian edition is entitled *Mussolini: piccolo borghese.*

7. *Ibid.,* pp. 84–86 and 106–11.

8. Emilio de Bono, *Anno XIIII: The Conquest of an Empire* (London, 1937), pp. 3ff.

9. Benito Mussolini, *The Fall of Mussolini* (New York, 1948), Max Ascoli, ed., p. 150.

10. *Ibid.,* p. 23.

11. Mario Toscano, "Introduction," in Pompeo Aloisi, *Journal, 1932–1936* (Paris, 1957), pp. x–xvi; Augusto Rosso, "Quattro momenti della diplomazia italiana," *Rivista di studi politici internazionali,* XXI (1954), 419–20.

12. Toscano, in Aloisi, *Journal*, p. xiv.

13. De Bono, *Anno XIIII*, pp. 13 and 26; Monelli, *Mussolini*, p. 137; Kurt von Schuschnigg, *Austrian Requiem* (New York, 1946), p. 114; Aloisi, *Journal*, p. 369. See also several personal letters from Ambassador Breckinridge Long in Rome to President Roosevelt, February 3, 8, and 15, 1935, Container 114, Long Papers, Library of Congress.

14. Ernest Work, *Ethiopia: A Pawn in European Diplomacy* (New Concord, Ohio, 1935), *passim*.

15. Pietro Badoglio, *The War in Abyssinia* (New York, 1937), p. 7.

16. Italian Minister Giuliano Cora, who had negotiated the Treaty with Haile Selassie, then Ras Tafari, contended later that it had secured positive results. It was not a question, Cora wrote, of Ethiopia's failing to live up to the Treaty, but of an abrupt reversal of Italian policy before the ink was dry. Giuliano Cora, "Il trattato italo-etiopico del 1928," *Rivista di studi politici internazionali*, XV (1948), 222–23.

17. Attilio Tamaro, *Venti anni di storia, 1922–1943* (Rome, 1954), III, 103 and 107.

18. Guido Leto, *OVRA* (Bologna, 1952), pp. 136–39.

19. Raffaele Guariglia, *Ricordi, 1922–1946* (Naples, 1950), p. 234.

20. William C. Askew, *Europe and Italy's Conquest of Libya* (Durham, N.C., 1942), *passim*.

21. Mussolini, *Fall*, p. 183. The text of Mussolini's plan is in Alessandro Lessona, *Memorie* (Florence, 1958), pp. 165ff.

22. Walters, *History of the League of Nations*, II, 628.

23. Aloisi, *Journal*, p. 247.

24. Hubert Lagardelle, *Mission à Rome: Mussolini* (Paris, 1955), pp. 109–10; D. C. Watt, "The Secret Laval-Mussolini Agreement of 1935 on Ethiopia," *Middle East Journal*, XV (1961), 77.

25. Lagardelle, pp. 273–87, exchange of letters between Mussolini and Laval in December 1935; Pierre Laval, *The Diary of Pierre Laval* (New York, 1948), p. 20.

26. Robert Vansittart, *The Mist Procession: The Autobiography of Lord Vansittart* (London, 1958), pp. 515–16; Guariglia, *Ricordi*, pp. 220–21; Fulvio Suvich in *Il processo Roatta* (Rome, 1945), p. 18. See also Watt's discussion, "The Secret Agreement," pp. 69–74.

27. John T. Marcus, *French Socialism in the Crisis Years, 1933–1936* (New York, 1958), p. 152; François Goguel, *La politique des partis sous la IIIe république* (Paris, 1958), pp. 405ff. The stories about Laval's trip to Rome are endless. Alexander Werth relates that it was pointed out to Laval after his agreement with Mussolini that Ethiopia after all was a member of the League of Nations. "Good God, is she really?" exclaimed Laval, much perturbed. Alexander Werth, *Which Way France?* (London, 1937), p. 100.

28. Charles A. Micaud, *The French Right and Nazi Germany, 1933–1939* (Durham, N.C., 1943), pp. 22–23.

29. *Parliamentary Debates, House of Commons* (London, 1935), Vol. 309, 5th Ser., Col. 275—hereafter referred to as *H.C. Debates*.

30. Guariglia, *Ricordi,* pp. 214–15.

31. *Ibid.,* pp. 217–18 and 231–32.

32. Geoffrey Thompson, *Front-Line Diplomat* (London, 1959), p. 95.

33. *H.C. Debates,* Vol. 309, Cols. 6–8.

34. Thompson, *Front-Line Diplomat,* pp. 104–6.

35. Charles L. Mowat, *Britain Between the Wars, 1918–1940* (London, 1955), p. 538.

36. Wolfgang Foerster, *Ein General kämpft gegen den Krieg* (Munich, 1949), p. 22; Hans-Heinrich Dieckhoff, Director of Department III of the German Foreign Ministry, to Willy Unverfehrt, Chargé in Addis Ababa, December 27, 1934, *Documents on German Foreign Policy,* Series C (1933–37), "The Third Reich: First Phase," III (Washington, D.C., 1959), p. 760; Bernhard von Bülow, State Secretary, to Ulrich von Hassell, Ambassador to Italy, March 26, 1935, *ibid.,* pp. 1083–84.

37. In a personal letter to Roosevelt on February 15, 1935, Ambassador Long in Rome noted that Italian factories were working day and night on military supplies and tropical equipment, that all Italian ports were making continued shipments of men and materials to East Africa, and that the two Italian colonies were importing large numbers of horses and mules from Canada and the United States. Long concluded that mules were no good on the flat coastal plains and could be intended only for mountain duty in the interior. Long Papers, Container 114, L.C.

38. Haile Selassie specifically asked for the application of Article 15 of the League Covenant concerning international disputes likely to lead to a rupture of relations between members.

39. Toscano, in Aloisi, *Journal,* p. xiii.

40. Thompson, *Front-Line Diplomat,* pp. 96–99; Vansittart, *Mist Procession,* p. 520; Thomas Jones, *A Diary With Letters, 1931–1950* (London, 1954), p. 187; Massimo Magistrati, "La Germania e l'impreso italiano di Etiopia," *Rivista di studi politici internazionali,* XVII (1950), 579.

41. *H.C. Debates,* Vol. 305, Col. 213.

42. Pierre-Etienne Flandin, *Politique française, 1919–1940* (Paris, 1947), p. 178.

43. *Il processo Roatta,* p. 19; Suvich used the English words "gentleman's agreement" in his statement.

44. Wilson to Hull, May 29, 1935, quoted in Hugh R. Wilson, Jr., *For Want of a Nail: The Failure of the League of Nations in Ethiopia* (New York, 1959), pp. 35–40.

45. Mowat, *Britain Between the Wars,* pp. 419ff. and 535.

46. Eugene J. Meehan, *The British Left Wing and Foreign Policy* (New Brunswick, N.J., 1960), pp. 39–40; Elaine Windrich, *British Labour's Foreign Policy* (Stanford, Calif., 1952), pp. 119ff. with quotations from "Socialism and Peace"; Henry Pelling, *America and the British Left* (London, 1956), pp. 146–48.

47. Clement R. Attlee, *As It Happened* (London, 1954), p. 98; Meehan, *British Left Wing*, pp. 40–41.

48. *H.C. Debates*, Vol. 302, Cols. 2194–95, 2201–2, and 2208–10.

49. Toynbee, *Abyssinia*, pp. 48ff.; Keith Feiling, *The Life of Neville Chamberlain* (London, 1947), p. 262; Robert Cecil, *A Great Experiment: An Autobiography* (London, 1941), *passim*; Paul Vaucher and Paul-Henri Siriex, *L'opinion britannique, la Société des Nations, et la guerre italo-éthiopienne* (Paris, 1936), pp. 31ff.

50. Toynbee, *Abyssinia*, pp. 48ff.

51. Vaucher and Siriex, *L'opinion britannique*, pp. 7–8 and 91–93.

52. Aloisi, *Journal*, pp. 271–72. For Eden's summation of Britain's dilemma, see Wilson to Hull, May 29, 1935, *For Want of a Nail*, pp. 35–40.

53. *H.C. Debates*, Vol. 312, Cols. 1991–92.

54. Aloisi, *Journal*, pp. 275–78.

55. *H.C. Debates*, Vol. 304, Col. 628; United States Ambassador Robert W. Bingham to Secretary of State Cordell Hull, July 16, 1935, State Department decimal files, National Archives, Washington, D.C.—hereafter referred to by sender to receiver with date.

56. *H.C. Debates*, Vol. 303, Col. 1522; 304:626–27.

57. Aloisi, *Journal*, pp. 282–83; Mario Toscano, "Eden a Roma alla vigilia del conflitto italo-etiopico," *Nuova antologia*, CCCCLXXVIII (January 1960), 33 and 43–44; Guariglia, *Ricordi*, p. 245. Amharic Ethiopia is the northwestern third of the country, traditional Abyssinia.

58. Aloisi, *Journal*, pp. 291–93.

59. *Ibid.*, pp. 293–97.

60. Walters, *History of the League of Nations*, II, 640.

61. Atherton to Hull, August 20 and 22, 1935; Marriner to Hull, August 19, 1935.

Chapter Two

1. Cf. Edwin Borchard and William P. Lage, *Neutrality for the United States* (New Haven, Conn., 1940), and Allen W. Dulles and Hamilton Fish Armstrong, *Can America Stay Neutral?* (New York, 1939).

2. Harold B. Hinton, *Cordell Hull: A Biography* (Garden City, N.Y., 1942), p. 281.

3. John Norman, "Influence of Pro-Fascist Propaganda on American Neutrality, 1935–1936," in Dwight E. Lee and George E. McReynolds, eds., *Essays in History and International Relations in Honor of George Hubbard Blakeslee* (Worcester, Mass., 1949), pp. 193–214 *passim*.

4. On isolationism, see especially Alexander DeConde, "On Twentieth-Century Isolationism," in DeConde, ed., *Isolation and Security* (Durham, N.C., 1957), pp. 16–24; John C. Donovan, "Congressional Isolationists and the Roosevelt Foreign Policy," *World Politics,* III (1951), 299–301; and Wayne S. Cole, *Senator Gerald P. Nye and American Foreign Relations* (Minneapolis, 1962), pp. 3–13.

5. Robert H. Ferrell, "The Peace Movement," in DeConde, ed., *Isolation, passim*; Elton Atwater, *Organized Efforts in the United States Toward Peace* (Washington, D.C., 1936), *passim.*

6. Allan Nevins, *The United States in a Chaotic World: A Chronicle of International Affairs, 1918–1933* (New Haven, Conn., 1950), pp. 5off.

7. Selig Adler, *The Isolationist Impulse* (New York, 1957), pp. 239–43.

8. *The Year of Crisis: 1933* (Vol. II of *The Public Papers and Addresses of Franklin D. Roosevelt,* compiled by Samuel I. Rosenman; New York, 1938), p. 547. The State Department drafted the President's speech, according to Cordell Hull, *The Memoirs of Cordell Hull* (New York, 1948), I, 387.

9. James MacGregor Burns, *Roosevelt: The Lion and the Fox* (New York, 1956), p. 247.

10. Arthur M. Schlesinger, Jr., *The Coming of the New Deal* (Boston, 1959), pp. 214ff; William E. Dodd, Jr., and Martha Dodd, eds., *Ambassador Dodd's Diary, 1933–1938* (New York, 1941), p. 208; Frances Perkins, *The Roosevelt I Knew* (New York, 1946), pp. 337ff.

11. Hull, *Memoirs,* I, 388.

12. Dodd, *Diary,* p. 208.

13. Whitney H. Shepardson and William O. Scroggs, *The United States in World Affairs, 1934–1935* (New York, 1935), pp. 224–26.

14. Dodd, *Diary,* p. 214; Harold L. Ickes, *The First Thousand Days, 1933–1936* (New York, 1953), pp. 284–85; Adler, *Isolationist Impulse,* pp. 255–56; Donovan, "Congressional Isolationists," p. 301.

15. See especially the exhaustive study of the arms embargo issue by Robert A. Divine, *The Illusion of Neutrality* (Chicago, 1962), pp. 1–121.

16. Hull, *Memoirs,* I, 398ff.

17. Divine, *Illusion of Neutrality,* pp. 81–121; Green to Davis, August 10, 1935, Container 26, Davis Papers, Library of Congress.

18. Hull, *Memoirs,* I, 406.

19. Franklin D. Roosevelt, *Press Conferences,* VI (July 24, 1935), 53–54; *New York Times,* July 25, 1935.

20. Arthur M. Schlesinger, Jr., *The Politics of Upheaval* (Boston, 1960), pp. 385ff.; Donovan, "Congressional Isolationists," p. 306.

21. Atherton to Hull, August 8, 1935.

22. Hull, *Memoirs,* I, 411.

23. Hull to Roosevelt, August 19, 1935.

24. Hull, *Memoirs*, I, 398; Wayne S. Cole, "Senator Key Pittman and American Neutrality Policies, 1933–1940," *Mississippi Valley Historical Review*, XLVI (1960), 644–62 *passim*.

25. Hull to Roosevelt, August 19, 1935; Memorandum from Pittman to Roosevelt, August 19, 1935; letter from Pittman to Early, August 19, 1935, all in Roosevelt Library.

26. Cole, *Senator Gerald P. Nye and American Foreign Relations*, pp. 104–5.

27. *New York Times*, August 23, 1935; Hull, *Memoirs*, I, 412; Divine, *Illusion of Neutrality*, pp. 112–13.

28. Hull, *Memoirs*, I, 414; Hull to Roosevelt, August 29, 1935.

29. Department of State, *Press Releases*, XIII (August 31, 1935), 162–63; *New York Times*, September 1, 1935.

30. Hull, *Memoirs*, I, 414; Memorandum by Green, September 10, 1935; "Background Information in Regard to the Recent Neutrality Legislation," State Department Information Series #96 (October 7, 1935); Divine, *Illusion of Neutrality*, pp. 116–17.

Chapter Three

1. Memorandum by Philip H. Alling of the State Department's Division of Near Eastern Affairs, December 28, 1934; "Ethiopia," State Department Information Series #69 (February 25, 1935).

2. George to Hull, December 13, 1934.

3. George to Hull, November 9, 1934.

4. Colonel J. G. Pillow to War Department, August 29 and September 21, 1934.

5. Bullitt to Hull, September 22, 1934.

6. Phillips to Jesse I. Straus in Paris, Robert W. Bingham in London, Long in Rome, and George, September 27, 1934.

7. Straus to Hull, October 12, 1934; Atherton to Hull, October 15, 1934; George to Hull, November 21, 1934.

8. Murray to Phillips, December 17, 1934; Memorandum by Alling, December 18, 1934.

9. George to Hull, December 19, 1934.

10. Hull to George, December 21, 1934.

11. Hull to George, July 5, 1935. The penciled changes appear to be in the President's handwriting.

12. George to Hull, July 15, 1935.

13. Hull to George, July 2, 1935; Engert to Hull, August 14, 1935; *New York Times*, July 8 and October 10, 1935.

14. Quoted in instructions from Phillips to Engert, July 22, 1935; Hull, *Memoirs*, I, 420.

15. Hull to George, July 10, 1935; Hull to Bingham, July 11, 1935.

16. Hull to Bingham, July 11, 1935; Phillips to Davis, July 11, 1935, Container 47, Davis Papers, Library of Congress.

17. Department of State, *Press Releases*, XIII (July 13, 1935), 53–54.

18. *New York Times*, July 6, 13, and 28, 1935. Under Secretary Phillips felt Hull's second statement had received a good reception in the press, and he noted that Hull had been in good spirits after glimpsing the *New York Times*. Phillips to Davis, July 13, 1935, Container 47, Davis Papers.

19. Engert to Hull, August 30, 1935.

20. Atherton to Hull, August 31, 1935; British Embassy Aide-Mémoire to Hull, August 31, 1935; *H.C. Debates*, Vol. 304, Cols. 156–57.

21. *New York Times*, September 1, 1935.

22. Murray to Hull, August 31, 1935; *New York Times*, September 1, 1935.

23. *New York Times*, August 31 and September 2 and 3, 1935. The September 2 issue carried a quip from the *London Financial Times*, September 1, 1935:

> A bold financier named Rickett,
> Booked to Addis Ababa a ticket;
>   Negus gave him oil,
>   Salt, pepper, and soil,
> But said Duce: "Queste non è cricket."

24. *New York Times*, September 2, 1935.

25. *Ibid.*, September 4 and 5, 1935; Memorandum by Murray, September 4, 1935.

26. Memorandum by Murray, September 4, 1935.

27. Engert to Hull, September 4, 1935.

28. Hull to Engert, September 5, 1935.

29. Roosevelt, *Press Conferences*, VI (September 4, 1935), 129–30.

30. Cf. Gaetano Salvemini, *Prelude to World War II* (London, 1953), p. 282. According to the famous anti-Fascist historian, the oil concession was a "concerted bombshell to discredit" Haile Selassie and to make Ethiopia appear ridiculous and Great Britain hypocritical.

31. *New York Times*, July 18, 1935. The National Peace Conference included, for example, the League of Nations Association, the Federal Council of Churches, and the Fellowship of Reconciliation.

32. *Christian Century*, LII (August 7, 1935), 1003 and 1006; (August 21, 1935), 1055; (September 4, 1935), 1099.

33. Abbe L. Warnshuis, Secretary of the International Missionary Council, to Murray, November 29, 1935.

34. *American Hebrew and Jewish Tribune*, CXXXVII (September 20, 1935), 311; *Jewish Frontier*, II (August 1935), 7–8.

35. *Commonweal*, XXII (May 3, 1935), 2.

36. *Pilot*, July 13, 1935.

37. *America,* LIII (July 20, 1935), 340–41; (September 7, 1935), 506; LIV (October 12, 1935), 3; *Commonweal,* XXII (July 12, 1935), 275; (August 20, 1935), 413; (October 4, 1935), 538; XXIII (November 1, 1935), 3; (November 8, 1935), 31.

38. *Opportunity,* XIII (August 1935), 231; *Crisis,* XLII (September 1935), 273.

39. *New York Times,* July 13 and 14, August 12 and 23, 1935; W. Randolph (alias), "The Communist Party of the United States," *Kommunisticheski Internatsional,* November 10, 1935, which the American Chargé in Riga, Latvia, forwarded to the State Department, April 10, 1936.

40. *New York Times,* August 15, 1935; *Christian Century,* LII (August 28, 1935), 1089; *Federal Council Bulletin,* XVIII (September 1935), 7; Memorandum by Alling, September 16, 1935.

Chapter Four

1. Benito Mussolini, *My Autobiography* (London, 1928), translated and with a foreword by Richard Washburn Child; Henry L. Stimson to the Editor, *New York Times,* October 11, 1935; Henry L. Stimson and McGeorge Bundy, *On Active Service in Peace and War* (New York, 1948), p. 269.

2. Roosevelt to John S. Lawrence, July 27, 1933, Roosevelt Library.

3. Louis A. DeSanti, "United States Relations with Italy Under Mussolini, 1922–1941" (Ph.D. dissertation, Columbia University, 1951), p. 217.

4. Rosso to Mussolini, June 25, 1935, Container 430, Captured Italian Documents, National Archives, Washington, D.C. Rosso's second point about the American sentiment against an active interest in European affairs is underlined in the Ministry's copy of the Ambassador's telegram.

5. Francesco Flora, *Stampa dell'era fascista* (Rome, 1945), p. 3; Leone Bortone, "Gli ordini alla stampa," *Il ponte,* VIII (October 1952), 1393–94. These two surveys, unfortunately, stress the period after the Italo-Ethiopian crisis.

6. E.g., "Il patriottismo degli Italiani d'America," *Il Giornale d'Italia,* July 20, 1935; "Plauso americano alla politica coloniale di Mussolini," *ibid.,* August 11, 1935.

7. *Il Corriere della Sera,* June 5, 1935.

8. Memorandum by Murray, February 14, 1935; Hull, *Memoirs,* I, 419.

9. Memorandum by Murray, April 27, 1935; Kirk to Hull, June 15, 1935; Murray to Phillips, June 17, 1935.

10. Kirk to Hull, July 12, 1935.

11. *La Tribuna,* July 7 and 9, 1935; *Il Corriere della Sera,* July 7, 1935, with the headline: "L'opinione pubblica americano approva la rapida

liquidazione dell'appello del Negus da parte del Governo de Washington."

12. *La Tribuna,* July 13, 1935; Kirk to Hull, July 12 and 17, 1935.

13. Kirk to Hull, July 26 and August 2 and 8, 1935. The article from *Il Popolo d'Italia* is quoted in the dispatch of August 2, 1935.

14. *Il Giornale d'Italia* or *Il Popolo d'Italia,* August 3, 1935. *Il Popolo* was Mussolini's newspaper, and *Il Giornale* was edited by Virginio Gayda, whom Ambassador Long thought the spokesman for the Italian Foreign Office and to whom Baron Aloisi often gave instructions. Long's diary, September 20, 1935, p. 209; Aloisi, *Journal,* p. 326 and *passim.*

15. *Il Giornale d'Italia,* August 12, 1935; Raffaele Guariglia, *Ricordi, 1922–1946* (Naples, 1950), p. 258; Rosso to Phillips, September 20, 1935.

16. Kirk to Hull, August 8, 1935.

17. Phillips to Atherton, July 31, 1935.

18. Hull to Atherton and Marriner, August 15, 1935.

19. Marriner to Hull, two telegrams, August 17, 1935.

20. Hull, *Memoirs,* I, 421–22; Hull to Kirk, August 18, 1935.

21. Kirk to Hull, August 19, 1935.

22. Memorandum from Roosevelt to Hull, August 20, 1935, Roosevelt Library. When Ambassador Long returned from his vacation, he wrote in his diary that the President's personal message had accomplished nothing because Italian determination was unshaken. Indeed, he said, had he been in Rome he would have advised against it. Long's diary, September 4, 1935, p. 191.

23. Kirk to Hull, August 17, 1935.

24. *Il Corriere della Sera,* August 20, 1935; *La Tribuna,* August 21, 1935.

25. "Report of the Bergamaschi Mission," Container 433, Captured Italian Documents, National Archives, Washington, D.C.; *New York Times,* August 26, 1935.

26. Long to Hull, September 4, 1935; *La Tribuna* and *Il Giornale d'Italia,* September 3–5, 1935.

27. Long to Hull, September 4, 1935.

28. Daniel Varé, *The Two Imposters* (London, 1949), p. 105.

29. "Report of Bergamaschi Mission."

30. In his report Bergamaschi specifically cited *The Road to War* (Boston, 1935) by Walter Millis.

31. "Report of Bergamaschi Mission." Italics in the original.

Chapter Five

1. Roosevelt to Norman Hapgood, August 28, 1935, Roosevelt Library.

2. Hull to Roosevelt, September 25, 1935.

158   NOTES TO PAGES 54–60

3. Harold L. Ickes, *The First Thousand Days, 1933–1936* (New York, 1953), pp. 445–46; *New York Times,* September 24 and 26, 1935.

4. Memorandum from Murray to Green, September 17, 1935.

5. Hull to Roosevelt, September 25, 1935.

6. William L. Langer and S. Everett Gleason, *The Challenge to Isolation, 1937–1940* (New York, 1952), pp. 4 and 9.

7. Department of State decimal files and original telegraph copies in the Roosevelt Library.

8. Green to Wilson, October 12, 1935, in Hugh R. Wilson, Jr., *For Want of a Nail: The Failure of the League of Nations in Ethiopia* (New York, 1959), pp. 28–29.

9. Stephen Heald, ed., *Documents on International Affairs, 1935* (London, 1937), II, 171.

10. Roosevelt to Hull, October 4, 1935, received 4:25 P.M.

11. Ickes, *Thousand Days,* p. 450; Robert E. Sherwood, *Roosevelt and Hopkins* (New York, 1950), I, 97.

12. Roosevelt to Storm, Roddan, and Stephenson, all of the Press Corps, October 4, 1935, Roosevelt Library. Ickes, in summarizing the entire trip in a diary entry of October 27, dated this suggested news release October 5.

13. Hull to Bingham, Straus, Long, Gilbert, and Engert, October 3, 1935.

14. Long to Hull, October 3 and 4, 1935; Bingham to Hull, October 4 and 5, 1935.

15. Green to Wilson, personal letter, October 12, 1935; Wilson, *For Want of a Nail,* pp. 28–29; Hull, *Memoirs,* I, 426–27; Herbert Feis, *Seen from E.A.* (New York, 1947), p. 230.

16. Hull to Wilson, October 4, 1935; Hull to Roosevelt, October 4, 1935.

17. Memorandum of telephone conversation between Hull and Wilson, October 5, 1935.

18. Hull to Roosevelt, October 5, 1935.

19. Roosevelt to Hull, October 5, 1935, received 3:20 P.M.; Hull to Roosevelt, October 5, 1935.

20. Roosevelt to Hull, October 5, 1935, received 4:45 P.M.; Hull to Roosevelt, October 5, 1935, sent 6:20 P.M. and received 6:34 P.M.

21. Sherwood, *Roosevelt and Hopkins,* p. 97; Roosevelt to Hull, October 5, 1935, sent 6:50 P.M. and received 9:50 P.M.

22. Wilson, *For Want of a Nail,* p. 29.

23. Hull to Roosevelt, October 5, 1935; Roosevelt to Hull, October 5, 1935, received 10:12 P.M.

24. Roosevelt to Hull, October 5, 1935, sent 9:45 P.M. and received October 6, 1935, 3:20 A.M.

25. Department of State, *Press Releases*, XIII (October 5, 1935), 255; Hull, *Memoirs*, I, 430.

26. Wilson to Hull, October 6, 1935.

Chapter Six

1. "Report of the Bergamaschi Mission," Container 433, Captured Italian Documents, National Archives, Washington, D.C.

2. *New York Times*, September 27, 1935.

3. Aloisi, *Journal*, p. 299. In a personal letter to President Roosevelt on September 6, Ambassador Breckinridge Long denied rumors which sought to explain Mussolini's uncompromising attitude by suggesting that he had lost his mind. Mussolini, he said, "has prepared for this situation through the last year and a half in a stealthy but deliberate manner." The Italians "are not mad. They are deliberate, determined, obdurate, ruthless, and almost vicious." Long to Roosevelt, September 6, 1935, Container 114, Long Papers.

4. Raffaele Guariglia, *Ricordi, 1922–1946* (Naples, 1950), pp. 241–42.

5. "Memorandum by the Italian Government on the Situation in Ethiopia," *League of Nations Publications, 1935* (Geneva, 1935), Vol. VII, No. 11, p. 63 and *passim*.

6. The *New York Times* reported (September 5, 1935) that the eight bulky packing cases filled with Aloisi's documentary evidence alleging Ethiopia's barbaric unfitness as a League member bore the label "Bologna."

7. Guariglia, *Ricordi*, pp. 265–69; Aloisi, *Journal*, pp. xv and 307.

8. "Records of the Sixteenth Ordinary Session of the Assembly," *League of Nations Official Journal*, Special Supplement No. 138 (Geneva, 1935), p. 46.

9. Herbert Feis, *Seen from E.A.* (New York, 1947), p. 206.

10. Memoranda from Hornbeck to Hull, September 11 and 12, 1935.

11. Department of State, *Press Releases*, XIII (September 14, 1935), 194–96.

12. "Records of the Sixteenth Ordinary Session of the Assembly," p. 44.

13. *Journal officiel, Débats parlementaires, Chambre des députés* (Paris, 1935), December 28, 1935, p. 2863.

14. *H.C. Debates*, Vol. 309, Col. 977.

15. Wilson to Hull, September 13, 1935.

16. *Ibid.*; Atherton to Hull, September 16, 1935.

17. Hull to Atherton, September 20, 1935.

18. Memorandum by Murray, September 20, 1935. Although this memorandum was originally Murray's, he revised it after discussions with Dunn and Hull.

19. Hull to Bingham, September 27, 1935.

20. Long to Hull, September 17, 1935. In this long conversation between the American Ambassador and the Italian Prime Minister, in which the latter spoke so bitterly about sanctions, Long had presented entirely on his own initiative a complex and startling proposal. Among suggestions of a more general European nature, Long's plan provided for the cession to Italy of the Ethiopian lowlands and the capital city of Addis Ababa. Nothing ever came of this curious proposal because both Mussolini and Hull rejected it outright, but it must have nevertheless reassured Mussolini that an American ambassador would even think of such a plan. Long to Hull, September 12 and 17, 1935.

21. Guariglia, *Ricordi*, p. 279.

22. *Opera omnia de Benito Mussolini* (Florence, 1960), XXVII, 158.

23. The Committee of Thirteen consisted of the Council minus Italy, which had lost its right to vote because it was directly involved in the dispute.

24. Wilson to Hull, October 12, 1935; Hugh R. Wilson, Jr., *For Want of a Nail: The Failure of the League of Nations in Ethiopia* (New York, 1959), pp. 48–54.

25. "Records of the Sixteenth Ordinary Session of the Assembly," pp. 113–14.

26. "Coordination Committee," *League of Nations Official Journal*, Special Supplement No. 145, *passim*.

27. Joint telegram to Mussolini from General Emilio de Bono, Marshal Pietro Badoglio, and Under Secretary for the Colonies Alexander Lessona, October 18, 1935, quoted in Emilio de Bono, *Anno XIIII: The Conquest of an Empire* (London, 1937), p. 275.

28. In a very significant letter to Colonel House concerning the April conference at Stresa, Roosevelt commented on a rumor that the Stresa powers might institute a naval blockade against Germany: "Such a blockade would raise for us the question of its effectiveness. If we found it was an effective blockade, as a matter of fact, recognition of the blockade by us would obviously follow. This, after all, is not a boycott nor an economic sanction, but in effect it is the same thing. A boycott or sanction could not be recognized by us without Congressional action but a blockade would fall under the Executive's power after establishment of the fact." Roosevelt to House, April 10, 1935, Roosevelt Library.

29. Winston S. Churchill, *The Gathering Storm* (Boston, 1948), pp. 176–77.

Chapter Seven

1. Memoranda by Green, Dunn, and Phillips, October 7, 1935; Wilson to Hull, October 8, 1935.

2. Long to Hull, October 15, 1935; Long's diary, October 14, 1935, p. 224.

3. Long to Hull, October 9, 1935.

4. Gilbert to Hull, October 8, 1935; Wilson to Hull, October 9, 1935; Hull to Gilbert, October 12, 1935; Hull, *Memoirs,* I, 431–32.

5. Herbert Feis, *Seen from E.A.* (New York, 1947), pp. 231–32.

6. Gilbert to Hull, October 15, 1935.

7. Hull to Gilbert, October 17, 1935.

8. Telephone conversation between Hull and Wilson, October 18, 1935.

9. Wilson to Hull, October 21, 1935.

10. *New York Times,* October 23, 1935.

11. Memorandum by Hornbeck, October 23, 1935; Feis, *Seen from E.A.,* p. 235.

12. Hull to Wilson, October 26, 1935; Hull, *Memoirs,* I, 434.

13. *New York Times,* October 28, 1935.

14. Roosevelt to Hull, October 10, 1935; Hull to Roosevelt, October 11, 1935, including Memorandum by Moore, October 10, 1935.

15. *New York Times,* October 11, 19, 24, 26, and 28, 1935.

16. State Department Memorandum of Hull's Press Conference, October 28, 1935; Roosevelt to Rev. W. Russell Bowie, October 30, 1935, Roosevelt Library.

17. Feis, *Seen from E.A.,* p. 256.

18. Hull to Roosevelt, October 11, 1935.

19. Raymond M. Schwartz to Roosevelt, October 7, 1935; *New York Times,* October 9, 1935.

20. Eleanor Clark, "The Italian Press, New York," *New Republic,* LXXXIV (November 6, 1935), 356–57.

21. Hull, *Memoirs,* I, 431; Department of State, *Press Releases,* XIII (October 12, 1935), 303–4.

22. Nye to Hull, October 16, 1935; *New York Times,* October 16, 1935.

23. Dunn to Davis, October 15, 1935, Davis Papers, Container 24, Library of Congress.

24. Memoranda by Feis, October 16 and 23, 1935.

25. Hull, *Memoirs,* I, 435; Roosevelt, *Press Conferences,* VI (October 30, 1935), 226; Department of State, *Press Releases,* XIII (November 2, 1935), 338–39.

26. Memorandum by Green, October 31, 1935.

27. Director of the Washington Office of the Institute of American Meat Packers to Hull, November 23, 1935; Green to Institute of American Meat Packers, December 5, 1935.

28. State Department Memorandum of Secretary's Press Conference, October 31, 1935.

29. Roosevelt, *Press Conferences,* VI (October 31, 1935), 227–28.

30. Feis, *Seen from E.A.,* p. 255.

31. Morgenthau to Roosevelt, October 7, 1935, Roosevelt Library.

32. Phillips to Long, October 5, 1935; Hull to Long and Engert, November 13, 1935.

33. Hull to J. R. Robinson, November 18, 1935.

34. Jefferson T. Coolidge, Under Secretary of the Treasury, to Phillips, October 5, 1935, and July 7, 1936; Phillips to Roosevelt, October 31, 1935; Harold L. Ickes, *The First Thousand Days, 1933–1936* (New York, 1953), p. 462.

35. Childs to Hull, November 2 and 4, 1935, with enclosure from the *Egyptian Gazette,* November 4, 1935.

36. Murray to Hull, November 4, 1935; Phillips to Childs, November 7, 1935.

37. *Il Corriere della Sera,* October 13, 1935.

38. *New York Times,* October 13, 1935.

39. Long to Hull, October 15, 1935; Memorandum by Phillips, October 16, 1935.

40. *La Tribuna,* October 8, 1935.

41. *Ibid.,* October 10, 1935.

42. *Il Giornale d'Italia,* October 30, 1935; *New York Times,* October 27, 1935; Long to Hull, October 29, 1935.

43. Memorandum by Chapin of the Division of Western European Affairs, October 10, 1935, on a dinner conversation with the Italian Ambassador.

44. Gilbert to Hull, November 4, 1935.

45. Hull, *Memoirs,* I, 435.

46. James A. Farley, *Jim Farley's Story* (New York, 1948), p. 56.

47. Department of State, *Press Releases,* XIII (November 16, 1935), 382.

48. Hull, *Memoirs,* I, 435–36.

49. Roosevelt to Hull, October 10, 1935.

50. Memorandum by Murray, November 15, 1935; *New York Times,* November 24, 1935.

51. *New York Times,* November 29, 1935.

52. James C. Peacock, Director of the Shipping Board Bureau, to John M. Johnson, Assistant Secretary of Commerce, November 4, 1935, enclosure to Memorandum by Phillips, November 12, 1935.

53. Jesse Jones, Chairman of the Reconstruction Finance Corporation, dismissed the possibility of using this same kind of financial pressure on the railroads as too impractical because of the difficulty of determining whether or not goods sent via rail were destined eventually for Italy. *New York Times,* November 26, 1935.

54. Peacock to Johnson, November 4, 1935, enclosure to Memorandum

by Phillips, November 12, 1935; Memorandum by Phillips, November 12, 1935, with handwritten note that Peacock had been informed, November 13, 1935.

55. To ensure a supply of the raw materials required by Italy, the Italian Embassy and Italian interests in the United States had themselves undertaken the purchase and export of American goods. They paid cash for the products at the place of manufacture and arranged for overseas shipment. Memorandum by Feis, November 4, 1935.

56. Memoranda by Green and Dunn, November 18, 1935.

57. Chapin to Dunn, November 20, 1935, with enclosures; Memorandum by Dunn, November 21, 1935.

58. Memoranda by Green, November 23 and 25, 1935; Memorandum by Moore, December 11, 1935.

59. Feis, *Seen from E.A.*, p. 304.

60. Memorandum by Dunn, November 5, 1935; Feis, *Seen from E.A.*, p. 256; "Fortune Quarterly Survey: III," *Fortune*, XIII (January 1936), 46–47. *Fortune* interviewers reported that "as the question was read, many people would begin by saying 'no' when they heard the words 'join other nations,' and then switch to 'yes' when they heard the complete question."

61. *New York Times*, November 7, 1935.

62. Long to Hull, November 6 and 7, 1935.

63. Long to Hull, November 8, 1935.

64. *La Stampa*, quoted in Long to Hull, November 14, 1935; *Il Giornale d'Italia*, November 10, 1935.

65. Louis A. DeSanti, "U.S. Relations with Italy Under Mussolini, 1922–1941" (Ph.D. dissertation, Columbia University, 1951), p. 250; Long to Hull, November 18, 1935; *The Times* (London), Rome correspondent, November 21, 1935.

66. Long to Hull, November 21, 1935; Long's diary, November 23 or 24, 1935, pp. 264–65.

67. Memorandum by Hull, November 22, 1935.

68. Memorandum by Green, November 22, 1935.

69. Roosevelt to Hull, November 27, 1935, Roosevelt Library.

70. *La Tribuna*, November 27, 1935.

71. *Ibid.*, November 26, 1935.

72. *Il Corriere della Sera*, December 3, 1935; *La Tribuna*, December 5, 1935.

Chapter Eight

1. Arnold J. Toynbee, *Abyssinia and Italy* (London, 1936), p. 276.

2. Timothy A. Taracouzio, *War and Peace in Soviet Diplomacy* (New York, 1940), pp. 193–95; Wladyslaw W. Kulski, *Peaceful Co-Existence:*

An Analysis of Soviet Foreign Policy (Chicago, 1959), pp. 139–41; Max Beloff, *The Foreign Policy of Soviet Russia, 1929–1941* (London, 1947), I, 91–92; address by Vladimir Potemkin, Alternate Representative of Russia, October 10, 1935, in "Records of the Sixteenth Ordinary Session of the Assembly," *League of Nations Official Journal*, Special Supplement No. 138 (Geneva, 1935), p. 107.

3. The point that the belief in American cooperation depended on one's attitude toward the League of Nations and Italy is further illustrated in memoirs of leading political figures. I have cited in the text only contemporary statements in the House of Commons, newspapers, or diaries. Compare, for example, Robert Cecil, *A Great Experiment: An Autobiography* (London, 1941), p. 275, and Leopold S. Amery, *My Political Life: The Unforgiving Years, 1929–1940* (London, 1955), pp. 140, 182, and 186.

4. *H.C. Debates,* Vol. 307, Cols. 324–28.

5. *Daily Herald,* November 20, 1935.

6. *News-Chronicle,* November 19 and 20, 1935.

7. Hoare related in his memoirs how he carried with him to Baldwin's country home a copy of the important speech planned for Geneva in mid-September: "When I arrived, we talked of the delights of Aix and the English countryside. We walked round the garden and we had tea. Then, remembering something about Geneva, he said to me: 'You have got a speech to make, and you have brought me the draft. Let me have a look at it.' When I gave it to him, he gave it a quick glance, and said, on handing it back to me: 'That is all right. It must have taken you a long time to make it up,' and that was all.... At least his perfunctory acquiescence showed confidence in his Foreign Secretary and enabled me to go ahead on the lines that I had set out." Samuel Hoare, *Nine Troubled Years* (London, 1954), p. 167.

8. *H.C. Debates,* Vol. 305, Col. 28.

9. *H.C. Debates,* Vol. 307, Cols. 343–44; Herbert Feis in *Seen from E.A.*, p. 251, cites only the first sentence of this quotation and thus gives the completely contrary impression that Great Britain questioned American cooperation.

10. *News-Chronicle,* December 6, 1935.

11. *H.C. Debates,* Vol. 307, Cols. 2008–9.

12. Keith Feiling, *The Life of Neville Chamberlain* (London, 1947), pp. 272 and 274.

13. *The Times,* November 25 and 29, 1935.

14. *Daily Telegraph,* December 2, 1935.

15. Wilson to Hull, November 30, 1935; Gilbert to Hull, November 29, 1935.

16. Aloisi, *Journal,* p. 324; Paul Schmidt, in R. H. C. Steed, ed., *Hitler's Interpreter* (New York, 1951), p. 60.

17. Alberto Berio, "L'*affare* etiopico," *Rivista di studi politici internazionali*, XXV (April–June 1958), 204. A spokesman for the Press Ministry in Rome stated that Cerruti had warned Laval that an oil embargo would be "an unfriendly act." (*Le Temps*, December 1, 1935.)

18. Aloisi, *Journal*, p. 303.

19. Marcus, *French Socialism in the Crisis Years, 1933–1936* (New York, 1958), pp. 155–56; Léon Blum, *L'histoire jugera* (Paris, 1945), pp. 101–2 and 107; *Le Populaire*, November 3, 5, and 26, 1935.

20. *Le Peuple*, November 24, 1935; *L'Humanité*, November 24 and 29, 1935.

21. Charles A. Micaud, *The French Right and Nazi Germany, 1933–1939* (Durham, N.C., 1943), pp. 2 and 50–65; François Goguël, *La politique des partis sous la IIIe république* (Paris, 1958), pp. 421–24. When ultimately this best-of-two-evils choice had to be made, as Mussolini betrayed the French right and scorned the apparently weak democracies for his Axis with Hitler, the right acquiesced in the appeasement of Germany. Rather Hitler than Léon Blum!

22. *Le Temps*, November 24 and 25, 1935; *Le Figaro*, November 26, 1935.

23. *Le Temps*, December 1, 1935; *Le Figaro*, November 29, 1935.

24. André François-Poncet, *The Fateful Years* (London, 1949), pp. 188–89.

25. Straus to Hull, November 25, 1935; Bingham to Hull, November 26, 1935; Long to Hull, November 26, 1935.

26. In response to a Havas dispatch that the United States had decided not to impose an oil embargo, Aloisi commented: "That would be good news!" Aloisi, *Journal*, p. 326.

27. Department of State Memorandum on Hull's Press Conference, November 26, 1935; see also *New York Times*, November 27, 1935.

28. Memorandum by Dunn, November 27, 1935.

29. Bingham to Hull, November 25 and 28, 1935; British Embassy to Department of State, Oral Communication, November 30, 1935.

30. "Communications Received from Certain Governments Regarding the Application of Article 16 of the Covenant (Mutual Support)," *League of Nations Official Journal*, Special Supplement No. 150 (Geneva, 1936), pp. 332–35.

31. *H.C. Debates*, Vol. 307, Cols. 65–66 and 342.

32. *Ibid.*, Col. 345.

33. Atherton to Hull, October 18, 1935; Bingham to Hull, October 19, 1935; Straus to Hull, October 29, 1935; Long to Hull, November 6, 1935.

34. Maurice Peterson, *Both Sides of the Curtain* (London, 1950), pp. 115–16; Vansittart, *The Mist Procession: The Autobiography of Lord Vansittart* (London, 1958), pp. 537–38.

35. Long to Hull, December 11, 1935; *Opera omnia di Benito Mussolini,* XXVII (Florence, 1960), 197.

36. *New York Times,* October 13, 1935.

37. Aloisi, *Journal, passim.*

38. Feiling, *Chamberlain,* p. 274.

39. *Ibid.,* pp. 272ff.; Hoare, *Troubled Years,* pp. 174ff.; Vansittart, *Mist Procession,* pp. 537ff.

40. Raffaele Guariglia, *Ricordi, 1922–1946* (Naples, 1960), pp. 291–94.

41. E.g., Toynbee, *Abyssinia,* pp. 312–13; *H.C. Debates,* Vol. 309, Cols. 101–2, by Arnold Wilson of his conversation with Il Duce; Guariglia, *Ricordi,* p. 297.

42. George M. Young, *Stanley Baldwin* (London, 1952), p. 217; *H.C. Debates,* Vol. 307, Col. 856.

43. *Ibid.,* Col. 2117.

44. *New York Times,* December 13, 1935; Memorandum by Borah, December 19, 1935, Borah Papers, Container 580, Library of Congress; Armstrong to Davis, telegram, December 13, 1935, Davis Papers, Container 2, Library of Congress; *Business Week,* No. 329 (December 21, 1935), 39.

45. Harold L. Ickes, *The First Thousand Days, 1933–1936* (New York, 1953), pp. 483–84.

46. *News-Chronicle,* December 16, 1935.

47. Toynbee, *Abyssinia,* p. 92.

48. Massimo Magistrati, "La Germania e l'impreso italiano di Etiopia," *Rivista di studi politici internazionali,* XVII (1950), 583–89.

49. *Ibid.,* pp. 590–92; Erich Kordt, *Nicht aus den Akten* (Stuttgart, 1950), p. 128.

50. Magistrati, "Germania," p. 595; Dodd to Hull, October 15, 1935.

51. Kordt, *Akten,* p. 128.

Chapter Nine

1. Pietro Badoglio, *The War in Abyssinia* (New York, 1947), Introduction by Mussolini, p. v.

2. A current joke viewed the Italo-Ethiopian conflict as a personal duel between Eden and Mussolini: "Without Eden, Mussolini would never have conquered Ethiopia. Without Mussolini, Eden would never have become Minister of Foreign Affairs." Massimo Magistrati, "La Germania e l'impreso italiano di Etiopia," *Rivista di studi politici internazionali,* XVII (1950), 587.

3. *Chambre des députés, Débats parlementaires, Journal officiel,* December 28, 1935, p. 2864.

4. *The Times* (London), January 3, 1936.

5. Henderson to Hull, December 30, 1935, and January 8, 1936.

6. Long to Hull, December 27, 1935.

7. *Il Giornale d'Italia,* January 3, 1936.

8. *La Tribuna,* January 4, 1936.

9. *The Public Papers and Addresses of Franklin D. Roosevelt,* compiled by Samuel I. Rosenman, V (New York, 1938), 8–12.

10. *New York Times,* January 5, 1936.

11. *Daily Mail,* January 6, 1936.

12. *Daily Herald* and *News-Chronicle,* January 4, 1936.

13. Quoted in *New York Times,* January 5, 1936, from editions of January 4, 1936; *Daily Mail,* January 6, 1936.

14. *News-Chronicle,* January 6, 1936; *Daily Herald,* January 7, 1936; see also *Manchester Guardian,* January 6 and 8, 1936.

15. *The Times* (London), January 6, 1936; see also *Daily Telegraph,* January 6, 1936.

16. *Le Temps,* January 5, 1936; *The Times* (London), January 6, 1936, review of Parisian press.

17. *Le Populaire* and *L'Humanité,* January 5 and 6, 1936.

18. Straus to Hull, January 9, 1936.

19. Roosevelt, *Public Papers,* V, 10.

20. *Il Giornale d'Italia,* January 7, 1936; *La Tribuna,* January 8, 1936.

21. Hull, *Memoirs,* I, 460–61.

22. Memoranda by Green, September 10 and 11 and November 20, 1935. Green was Chief of the Division of Western European Affairs until late September, when he became head of the Office of Arms and Munitions Control.

23. Harold L. Ickes, *The First Thousand Days, 1933–1936* (New York, 1953), p. 483.

24. Moore to Newton D. Baker, December 13, 1935, Moore Papers, Roosevelt Library; Hull, *Memoirs,* I, 461ff; Robert A. Divine, *The Illusion of Neutrality* (Chicago, 1962), pp. 136–37.

25. Roland N. Stromberg, "American Business and the Approach of War, 1935–1941," *The Journal of Economic History,* XIII (Winter 1953), 61–67.

26. Gaetano Salvemini, "Mussolini's Empire in the United States," in Frances Keene, ed., *Neither Liberty Nor Bread: The Meaning and Tragedy of Fascism* (New York, 1940), p. 338; Massimo Salvadori, *Resistenza ed azione* (Bari, 1951), pp. 162–63.

27. John Norman, "Influence of Pro-Fascist Propaganda on American Neutrality, 1935–36," in Dwight E. Lee and George E. McReynolds, eds., *Essays in History and International Relations in Honor of George Hubbard Blakeslee* (Worcester, Mass., 1949), pp. 212–13; *Atlantica,* XVII (October 1935), 357. The editors of *Atlantica* offered as a special inducement to new subscribers "A Brand New Map of Ethiopia."

28. Memorandum by Yost, Office of Arms and Munitions Control, De-

168

NOTES TO PAGES 124–29

cember 21, 1935; letter from State Department Special Agent to Green, January 6, 1936. *Il Progresso* adopted the form letter because those who were most enthusiastic often could not read English.

29. *Atlantica,* XVIII (February 1936), 36.

30. Moore to the Secretary of the Italian Red Cross Committee of the Italian Chamber of Commerce of Queens and the United Italian Societies of Long Island, December 26, 1935; Moore to Roosevelt, January 23, 1936, Moore Papers; Memorandum by Moore, January 31, 1936, Moore Papers.

31. "The World As Seen Through the Eyes of the Italian Foreign Office, The United States—1936," Container 1291, Captured Italian Documents, National Archives, Washington, D.C. See also *Atlantica,* XVIII (February 1936), 45; Norman, "Influence of Pro-Fascist Propaganda," p. 213.

32. *New York Times,* January 11, 1936; Memorandum on Proposed Neutrality Act of 1936, n.d. [January 1936?], Borah Papers, Container 580, Library of Congress.

33. *Daily Mail, Daily Herald,* and *News-Chronicle,* January 13, 1936. The *Daily Mail* also printed a not very subtle cartoon picturing Washington cutting down the cherry tree of sanctions: "I cannot tell a lie. I did it with my little hatchet," while "jingo-pacifist," "warmonger," and "screaming sanctionist" wept copiously.

34. *Daily Telegraph,* January 20 and 27, 1936.

35. *Le Populaire,* January 14 and 20, 1936; *Le Temps,* January 13, 1936; *Le Figaro,* January 14, 1936.

36. *Il Giornale d'Italia,* January 12, 1936; *La Tribuna,* January 14, 1936.

37. Gilbert to Hull, January 17, 1936.

38. *New York Times,* January 5 and February 23, 1936. The January 5 article by the military analyst Captain B. H. Liddell Hart was almost a direct quotation from a January 4 editorial in *The Times* (London).

39. "Committee of Eighteen," *League of Nations Official Journal,* Special Supplement No. 148 (Geneva, 1936), pp. 7–9.

40. Ickes, *Thousand Days,* p. 533; Hull, *Memoirs,* I, 465.

41. Memorandum by Moore, n.d. [early February 1936?], Moore Papers; Hull, *Memoirs,* I, 465.

42. Memorandum by Alling, January 16, 1936; "The Military Situation in Ethiopia," War Department to Phillips, February 8, 1936; Atherton to Hull, January 18, 1936; Gilbert to Hull, February 6, 1936.

43. Department of State, *Press Releases,* XIV (March 7, 1936), 198.

44. "Report of the Committee of Experts," *League of Nations Publications, General, 1936* (Geneva, 1936), No. I, p. 5.

45. *H.C. Debates,* Vol. 309, Col. 151; see also *News-Chronicle,* February 10, 14, and 25, 1936.

46. *Daily Mail,* February 14, 1936; *H.C. Debates,* Vol. 309, Cols. 98 and 129–30; Leopold S. Amery, *My Political Life: The Unforgiving Years, 1929–1940* (London, 1955), p. 186.

47. *H.C. Debates,* Vol. 309, Cols. 76–87.

48. *Daily Telegraph,* February 13, 1936; *The Times* (London), February 18, 1936.

49. *L'Humanité,* February 8 and 15, 1936; *Le Populaire,* February 23 and 26, 1936.

50. *Le Temps,* February 10 and 19 and March 2, 1936; *Le Figaro,* February 4, 1936.

51. *La Tribuna* and *Il Giornale d'Italia,* February 20, 1936; *Opera omnia di Benito Mussolini,* XXVII (Florence, 1960), 232–33.

52. "The United States: 1936," Captured Italian Documents.

Chapter Ten

1. *New York Times,* March 5, 1936.

2. Alberto Berio, "L'affare etiopico," *Rivista di studi politici internazionali,* XXV (April–June 1958), 208–9; Long to Hull, March 2, 1936, on a similar conversation between Mussolini and French Ambassador Chambrun.

3. Gilbert to Hull, March 2, 1936.

4. "Committee of Eighteen," *League of Nations Official Journal,* Special Supplement No. 149 (Geneva, 1936), pp. 12–13.

5. Wilson to Hull, March 4, 1936.

6. *New York Times,* March 4, 1936, by correspondent George Steer.

7. Paul Schmidt, in R. H. C. Steed, ed., *Hitler's Interpreter* (New York, 1951), p. 40; André François-Poncet, *The Fateful Years* (London, 1949), p. 189.

8. Gilbert to Hull, April 11 and 15, 1936; Bingham to Hull, April 14 and 15, 1936.

9. Aloisi, *Journal,* p. 377.

10. Gilbert to Hull and Wilson to Hull, April 20, 1936.

11. *H.C. Debates,* Vol. 310, Cols. 2458 and 2461–62.

12. *Ibid.,* Cols. 2507–8.

13. *New York Times,* April 18, 1936.

14. *H.C. Debates,* Vol. 310, Col. 3057.

15. *Ibid.,* Cols. 1746 and 1837.

16. *Ibid.,* Vol. 311, Cols. 534–35.

17. *Opera omnia di Benito Mussolini,* XXVII (Florence, 1960), 269.

18. *New York Times,* May 6, 1936.

19. Keith Feiling, *The Life of Neville Chamberlain* (London, 1947), p. 296; *H.C. Debates,* Vol. 313, Cols. 401–3.

20. *Ibid.,* Cols. 1198–1200.

21. "Records of the Sixteenth Ordinary Session of the Assembly," *League of Nations Official Journal,* Special Supplement No. 151 (Geneva, 1935), p. 65.

22. Roper to Hull, May 28, 1936; Memorandum by Green, June 17, 1936.

23. "The United States–1936," Container 1291, Captured Italian Documents, National Archives, Washington, D.C.

24. Engert to Hull, May 2, 1936.

25. Hull to Engert, May 9, 1936; Hull to Kirk, May 16, 1936.

26. Engert to Hull, June 5, 1936; Kirk to Hull and Hull to Roosevelt, June 12, 1936; General Rodolfo Graziani, who had replaced Badoglio in late May as Italian Commander-in-Chief in East Africa, painted the same picture that Engert had reported to Washington. Emilio Canevari, *Graziani mi ha detto* (Rome, 1947), p. 19.

27. Engert to Hull, June 18, 1936.

28. Hull to Roosevelt, June 19, 1936, with enclosure from Legal Adviser Hackworth, May 25, 1936, Roosevelt Library.

29. *H.C. Debates,* Vol. 313, Col. 1625.

Conclusion

1. William Phillips, *Ventures in Diplomacy* (North Beverly, Mass., 1952), p. 179.

2. "The United States–1936," Container 1291, Captured Italian Documents, National Archives, Washington, D.C.

3. Phillips, *Ventures,* p. 199.

4. William L. Langer and S. Everett Gleason, *The Challenge to Isolation, 1937–1940* (New York, 1952), pp. 77–78; Sumner Welles, Memorandum of Conversation between Roosevelt and Colonna, March 22, 1939, Roosevelt Library; cf. Roosevelt's appeal to Mussolini in August 1935 on the eve of the Italian invasion of Ethiopia.

5. World Peace Foundation, *Documents of American Foreign Relations, 1938–1939* (Boston, 1939), pp. 306–9 and 325–26.

6. "The United States–1937," Container 1290, Captured Italian Documents; Chargé Reed to Hull, November 17, 1938, quoting a comment by Italian spokesman Virginio Gayda; Roosevelt to Henry A. Wallace, April 14, 1939, quoted in Langer and Gleason, *Challenge,* p. 88; Burns, *Roosevelt: The Lion and the Fox* (New York, 1956), p. 385.

7. *The Public Papers and Addresses of Franklin D. Roosevelt,* compiled by Samuel I. Rosenman, IX (New York, 1938), 259ff.

Bibliographical Note

The Bibliographical Note briefly describes the books, articles, and other source materials that were most pertinent to my study of the Italo-Ethiopian crisis. It is divided into six sections: General, United States, Italy, Great Britain, France, and Miscellaneous.

General

Still the most complete history of the Italo-Ethiopian crisis is Arnold J. Toynbee, *Abyssinia and Italy*, the second volume of the Royal Institute of International Affairs, *Survey of International Affairs: 1935* (London, 1936). The Royal Institute's companion volume, *Documents on International Affairs: 1935* (London, 1937), II, edited by Stephen Heald, is a valuable collection of public documents and important speeches. Whereas Toynbee is almost encyclopedic, Francis P. Walters, "The Italo-Ethiopian War," *A History of the League of Nations* (London, 1952), II, 623–91, is very concise. Walters, formerly a Deputy Secretary General of the League, considers the Italo-Ethiopian crisis "the most important and most decisive chapter in the history of the League." Alberto Berio, an Italian on the staff of the League secretariat, has an objective but not very revealing article, "L'affare etiopico," *Rivista di studi politici internazionali*, XXV (April–June 1958), 181–219.

An excellent contemporary monograph on the League of Nations, which rightfully stresses the political rather than the technical background for the failure of sanctions, is Albert E. Highley, *The Actions of the States Members of the League of Nations in Applications of Sanctions Against Italy 1935–1936* (Geneva, 1938). Also dealing with sanctions is the Royal Institute of International Affairs, *International Sanctions* (London, 1938). Among the more useful French theses on sanctions and the League are Pierre Bartholin, *Aspects économiques des sanctions prises contre l'Italie* (Paris, 1938); Jean Bastin, *L'affaire d'Ethiopie et les diplomates (1934–1937)* (Paris, 1937); Léon-Jean Cibot, *L'Ethiopie et la Société des Nations* (Paris, 1939); Armand Cohen, *La Société des Na-*

tions devant le conflit italo-éthiopien (Décembre 1934–Octobre 1935) (Geneva, 1960); and Eugène-Louis Leroux, *Le conflit italo-éthiopien devant la SDN* (Paris, 1937). The *League of Nations Official Journal* and *Publications* are basic sources for the formal activities and resolutions of the League.

In a class by itself as an interpretation of the Italo-Ethiopian crisis is Gaetano Salvemini, *Prelude to World War II* (London, 1953). Salvemini, a prominent anti-Fascist Italian historian and a bitter foe of Mussolini, concludes that British leadership intentionally deceived the people over the farce of sanctions. His argument relies heavily on selective newspaper accounts and rumors.

United States

The diplomatic correspondence, interdepartmental communications, and memoranda of the State Department are located in the Foreign Affairs Branch of the National Archives. The bulk of the material on the Italo-Ethiopian controversy is recorded or cross-indexed under decimal file number 765.84, which designates the political relations of Italy with Ethiopia. There are other files of interest on peripheral subjects, such as 711.00111, Armaments Control, or 884.6363, African Exploration and Development Corporation. As an aid in locating documents on a specific phase of the dispute, the State Department has prepared *An Auxiliary Record of the Italo-Ethiopian Controversy*, a special purport book divided according to 39 topics rather than chronologically by decimal file number. The several volumes of *Foreign Relations of the United States, 1934–1937* (Washington, D.C., 1951–54) contain many of the basic documents. The decimal files include the Italo-Ethiopian crisis under the Italian file number while the published documents list the controversy under "Ethiopia"! The *Press Releases* of the State Department, XII–XIII (Washington, D.C., 1935–36), contain all the statements and speeches of the President and the Secretary of State.

The State Department records are excellent for determining what the government learned from its representatives abroad and what action it took, but these records are very limited in notes, memoranda, etc., which might indicate why and how the government made a particular decision or took a specific action. Helpful in filling this gap are the files and letters of President Roosevelt and the memoirs of other government officials. The Franklin D. Roosevelt Library at Hyde Park, New York, has the President's several files and the papers of Assistant Secretary of State R. Walton Moore. Much of the material at Hyde Park pertaining to the Italo-Ethiopian crisis duplicates the State Department decimal files. It does, however, include several interesting collections, such as the original telegrams between Roosevelt and Hull on application of the neutrality embargo, various neutrality drafts and memoranda in the Moore papers, and the personal letters of the President. Some of these letters are included in Elliott Roosevelt's edition of *F.D.R.: His Personal Letters, 1928–1945* (New York, 1950), I. Stenographic transcripts of the President's press conferences are also available at the Roosevelt Library. Samuel Rosenman has compiled the more important statements, papers, and addresses in *The Public Papers and Addresses of Franklin D. Roosevelt* (New York, 1938–50), in 13 volumes.

The papers of Norman H. Davis are the most useful of the collections of personal files available in the Manuscript Division of the Library of Congress. During 1935, between his assignments as American representative at the Geneva Disarmament Conference and as head of the American delegation to the London Naval Conference, Davis returned to the United States for a rest. His friends in the State Department, Division Chiefs James Dunn and Joseph C. Green, kept him informed of the activities and opinions of the Department. The papers of Cordell Hull have little on the Italo-Ethiopian crisis beyond material already available in the State Department's decimal files or in the Roosevelt Library. The papers of Breckinridge Long repeat material contained in his regular reports to the State Department, but in a few cases the comments in his dairy or in his many personal letters to Roosevelt are quite interesting and frank. The papers of Senators Tom Connally and Key Pittman, leading members of the Senate Foreign Relations Committee, are disappointing. The voluminous and loosely organized files of Senator William E. Borah have much on the neutrality issue during the late 1930's but little on the years 1935–36.

The bulk of the memoirs covering Roosevelt's first term deal almost exclusively with internal problems. The most useful of these is Harold L. Ickes, *The Secret Diary of Harold L. Ickes*, I, *The First Thousand Days, 1933–1936* (New York, 1953), which clearly indicates the personal feelings of the President and notes pertinent discussions in several Cabinet meetings with regard to the Italo-Ethiopian crisis. The best secondary sources for the domestic background in 1935 and 1936 are Arthur M. Schlesinger, Jr., *The Coming of the New Deal* (Boston, 1959), and *The Politics of Upheaval* (Boston, 1960), the second and third volumes of Schlesinger's *Age of Roosevelt*. James MacGregor Burns, *Roosevelt: The Lion and the Fox* (New York, 1956), is a bit severe on Roosevelt's handling of the Italo-Ethiopian crisis.

Of the diplomatic memoirs the most important is Cordell Hull, *The Memoirs of Cordell Hull* (New York, 1948), I, which is based on the State Department files and which favorably examines the Secretary of State's policies with a touch of hindsight. A dated and inadequate biography of the Secretary is Harold B. Hinton, *Cordell Hull: A Biography*

(Garden City, N.Y., 1942). Other valuable memoirs or collections are William E. Dodd, *Ambassador Dodd's Diary, 1933–1938* (New York, 1941),
edited by William E. Dodd, Jr. and Martha Dodd; Herbert Feis, *Seen
from E.A.* (New York, 1947); Hugh Wilson, Jr., *For Want of a Nail: The
Failure of the League of Nations in Ethiopia* (New York, 1959). Dodd was
Ambassador to Germany. Feis's book is a series of lectures, one of which,
entitled "Oil for Italy: A Study in the Decay of International Trust," was
based largely on the author's experiences as the State Department's
International Economic Adviser. Feis takes a cynical view of American
policy in the Italo-Ethiopian crisis. Wilson's background chapters are
superficial, but the accompanying personal letters of his father, the
American Minister to Switzerland, to various officials of the State Department and the memoranda of conversations between his father and
European diplomats are valuable. William Phillips, *Ventures in Diplomacy* (North Beverly, Mass., 1952), adds little new information, which
is unfortunate since Phillips was Under Secretary of State during the
Italo-Ethiopian crisis and Ambassador to Italy following it.

A good introduction to American diplomatic history in the twentieth
century is Foster Rhea Dulles, *America's Rise to World Power, 1898–1954*
(New York, 1954), which stresses the conflict between the isolationist
tradition and the newer concept for American participation in international affairs. More detailed on recent American diplomacy is Richard
W. Leopold, *The Growth of American Foreign Policy* (New York, 1962).

Several short articles deal specifically with the United States and the
Italo-Ethiopian crisis: Henderson B. Braddick, "A New Look at American Policy During the Italo-Ethiopian Crisis, 1935–36," *Journal of Modern History,* XXXIV (March 1962), 64–73; Robert A. Friedlander, "New
Light on the Anglo-American Reaction to the Ethiopian War, 1935–
1936," *Mid-America,* XLV (April 1963), 115–25; and Raimondo Manzini,
"Le leggi di neutralità degli Stati Uniti d'America (1793–1941)," *Rivista
di studi politici internazionali,* XXIII (January–March 1956), 28–70.
Braddick interprets Hull's support for Britain against Italy in the context
of the Secretary's desire for Anglo-American cooperation in the Pacific.
Manzini, an official of the Italian Ministry of Foreign Affairs, views
American neutrality policy in the Italo-Ethiopian crisis as informal dis-
crimination against Italy in support of the League. See also the annual
series *1934–1935* and *1936, The United States in World Affairs* (New
York, 1935 and 1937), by Whitney H. Shepardson and William O.
Scroggs, good contemporary accounts of the American role in the Italo-
Ethiopian crisis from an internationalist viewpoint. Relying almost
exclusively on State Department files, Louis A. DeSanti views the crisis
as a turning point in Italian-American relations in "U.S. Relations With
Italy Under Mussolini: 1922–1941" (Ph.D. dissertation, Columbia University, 1951).

Specifically on isolationism and on American attitudes toward foreign relations are Selig Adler, *The Isolationist Impulse* (New York, 1957); Robert E. Osgood, *Ideals and Self-Interest in America's Foreign Relations* (Chicago, 1953); and Alexander DeConde, "On Twentieth Century Isolationism," *Isolation and Security* (Durham, N.C., 1957), pp. 3–32. Robert A. Divine, *The Illusion of Neutrality* (Chicago, 1962), exhaustively treats the arms embargo issue during the decade before America entered the Second World War. Wayne S. Cole stresses the agricultural basis for isolationism in *Senator Gerald P. Nye and American Foreign Relations* (Minneapolis, 1962) and the important role played by the semi-isolationist Senator Pittman in the neutrality legislation of 1935–36 in "Senator Key Pittman and American Neutrality Policies, 1933–1940," *Mississippi Valley Historical Review*, XL (March 1960), 644–62. The struggle between isolationists and internationalists, though vitally important during the Italo-Ethiopian crisis, reached its peak in the late 1930's, and most of the literature stresses events after 1935–36. Contrast, for example, Edwin M. Borchard and William P. Lage, *Neutrality for the United States* (New Haven, Conn., 1937), with Allen W. Dulles and Hamilton Fish Armstrong, *Can America Stay Neutral?* (New York, 1939).

An excellent discussion of Roosevelt, Hull, and the making of American foreign policy is in the introductory chapter of William L. Langer and S. Everett Gleason, *The Challenge to Isolation, 1937–1940* (New York, 1952). John C. Donovan, "Congressional Isolationists and the Roosevelt Foreign Policy," *World Politics*, III (April 1951), 299–316, is a brief but good evaluation of the President's leadership in foreign affairs. Less sympathetic to Rooseveltian diplomacy are Charles A. Beard, *American Foreign Policy in the Making, 1932–1940* (New Haven, Conn., 1948), and Charles C. Tansill, *Back Door to War* (Chicago, 1952). Beard, relying on selective quotations and ignoring domestic political considerations, characterizes Roosevelt as a determined isolationist. Tansill, on the other hand, criticizes the administration's efforts to cooperate or to consult with other nations by means of the Kellogg-Briand Pact or the League of Nations. All of these, however, emphasize the period following the Italo-Ethiopian crisis.

Public opinion polling had only begun in the 1930's. Neither Hadley Cantril's compilation of polling statistics, *Public Opinion, 1935–1946* (Princeton, N.J., 1951), nor *Public Opinion Quarterly* includes any data on the American response to the Italo-Ethiopian crisis. Two relevant polls are noted briefly in *Fortune*, "Fortune Quarterly Survey," XIII (January 1936), 46–47, and in George Gallup, "What We, the People, Think about Europe," *New York Times Magazine*, April 30, 1939. A contemporary monograph on international public opinion including the United States is Helen Hiett, "Public Opinion and the Italo-Ethiopian Dispute," *Geneva Special Studies*, Vol. 7, No. 1 (February 1936).

The attitudes of specific groups as representative of public sentiment and their activities in seeking to influence opinion are shown in articles in the *New York Times* and letters to the Department of State. In addition, I examined *America* (Jesuit weekly); *American Hebrew and Jewish Tribune; Atlantica* (Italian-American); *Christian Century* (nondenominational Protestant); *Commonweal* (liberal Catholic); *Crisis* (National Association for the Advancement of Colored People); *Jewish Frontier* (Zionist); *Opportunity* (National Urban League); *Pilot* (Catholic Archdiocese of Boston); and *Il Progresso Italo-Americano* (pro-Fascist Newark, New Jersey, daily). Roland N. Stromberg has an excellent review of business attitudes toward neutrality in "American Business and the Approach of War, 1935–1941," *Journal of Economic History*, XIII (Winter 1953), 58–78. *Business Week, Commercial and Financial Chronicle,* and *American Exporter* are representative business publications with considerable comment on neutrality and the Italo-Ethiopian crisis. *National Petroleum News* is especially interesting on the views of American oil companies. Specifically on the peace movement are two excellent and concise accounts, a contemporary monograph and a recent article: Elton Atwater, *Organized Efforts in the United States Toward Peace* (Washington, D.C., 1936), and Robert H. Ferrell, "The Peace Movement," *Isolation and Security* (Durham, N.C., 1957), edited by Alexander DeConde, pp. 82–106.

There are several penetrating essays on the position of Italian-Americans and the efforts of Italian propagandists in the United States. The most useful, because it deals exclusively with the Italo-Ethiopian crisis, is an essay by John Norman, "Influence of Pro-Fascist Propaganda on American Neutrality, 1935–1936," *Essays in History and International Relations in Honor of George Hubbard Blakeslee* (Worcester, Mass., 1949), edited by Dwight E. Lee and George E. McReynolds, pp. 193–214. On the Italian-American response to Fascist Italy in the 1930's, see Gaetano Salvemini, "Mussolini's Empire in the United States," *Neither Liberty Nor Bread: The Meaning and Tragedy of Fascism* (New York, 1940), edited by Francis Keene, pp. 336–49, and Massimo Salvadori, *Resistenza ed azione* (Bari, 1951). The English edition of Salvadori's work, entitled *The Labour and the Wounds* (London, 1958), is shorter, and unfortunately excludes some of the author's comments on Italian-Americans.

Italy

Since the end of the Second World War, democratic Italy has been fascinated with uncovering all possible information about its Fascist era. Emiliano P. Noether, "Italy Reviews Its Fascist Past: A Bibliographical Essay," *American Historical Review*, LXI (July 1956), 877–99, is an excellent survey of the postwar decade of Italian historical literature on all phases of Fascism. Specifically on Mussolini is Elio Festa, "I biografi di Mussolini," *Nuova rivista storica*, XLV (September–December 1961), 467–513.

The diplomatic papers of the Italian Ministry of Foreign Affairs are in the process of arrangement and publication. Unfortunately, the documents already in print from the seventh and eighth series, 1922–35 and 1935–39, are from the first years of the first period and the last years of the second. Mario Toscano, the Italian historian who is editing the 1935–39 series, has published several articles based on these records. Of particular interest is his documentary article, "Eden a Roma alla vigilia del conflitto italo-etiopico," *Nuova antologia*, CCCCLXXVIII (January 1960), which debunks the myth of a fierce and dramatic encounter between Eden and Mussolini.

Some documents from the Italian Foreign Ministry captured at the close of the Second World War are available on microfilm in the Foreign Affairs Branch of the National Archives in Washington. Although incomplete and neither systematically arranged nor indexed, the captured Italian records are quite useful; especially interesting are scattered communications from the Embassy in Washington to the various ministers in Rome, records of the Bergamaschi Mission, and an annual series entitled "The World As Seen Through the Eyes of the Italian Foreign Office." The Foreign Office report, a group of secret reports from Italian diplomats abroad on the political situation in their respective countries, is available for the United States only for the year 1936.

Contemporary Italian newspapers provide an additional source of information on Italian policy with respect to the United States and the Italo-Ethiopian crisis. Francesco Flora, *Stampa dell'era fascista* (Rome, 1945), and Leone Bartone, "Gli ordini alla stampa," *Il ponte*, VIII (October 1952), 1393–402, indicate how strictly the government regulated the Italian press, which always placed Italy in the most favorable light and selected news about the United States and other countries accordingly. Unfortunately, these two collections of daily directives from Mussolini and the Ministry of Popular Culture to the Italian press derive mainly from the late 1930's.

Editorials by Virginio Gayda in *Il Giornale d'Italia* and Roberto Davanzati Forges in *La Tribuna* were particularly authoritative. Gayda was reputed to be a spokesman for the Italian Foreign Ministry, and Forges was a Fascist senator. The Library of Congress in Washington has almost complete files for 1935 and 1936 of *Il Corriere della Sera* (Milan), *Il Giornale d'Italia* (Rome), and *La Tribuna* (Rome). I have also occasionally cited *La Stampa* (Turin) and Mussolini's own newspaper, *Il Popolo d'Italia* (Rome and Milan). *Il Giornale d'Italia* had the most extensive coverage of American news.

Since the Second World War, Italian magazines have published large numbers of documents, secondary articles, and semi-memoirs on Italy's Fascist past. The most important is *Rivista di studi politici internazionali,* but other historical journals and more popular and literary magazines are also valuable. *Il ponte,* for instance, devoted the entire October 1952 issue to "Fascism, Thirty Years After," including an interesting article on Fascist imperialism on the eve of the Italo-Ethiopian crisis by Maurice Vaussard, "Il periodo ascendente dell'imperialismo fascista." Vaussard has included this as a chapter in his recent study of Italian nationalism, *De Pétrarque à Mussolini: évolution du sentiment nationaliste italien* (Paris, 1961).

Although the available Italian diplomatic documents and the controlled Italian press expressed considerable interest and concern over the American response to the Italo-Ethiopian crisis, this reaction is almost totally lacking in the many memoirs of the Fascist period. The most important and least argumentative, but containing little mention of the United States, are Pompeo Aloisi, *Journal* (Paris, 1957), with a valuable though charitable introduction by Mario Toscano, and Raffaele Guariglia, *Ricordi, 1922–1946* (Naples, 1950). Baron Aloisi was Italian Delegate to the League of Nations and Foreign Ministry Cabinet Chief; Guariglia, like Aloisi a career diplomat, served in 1935–1936 as the Foreign Ministry's Ethiopian expert. Under Secretary of State Fulvio Suvich has left no published memoirs, and the testimony at his postwar trial is disappointing in *Il processo Roatta* (Rome, 1945).

Other memoirs of interest for Italy's Ethiopian venture are Emilio de Bono, *Anno XIIII: The Conquest of an Empire* (London, 1937); Pietro Badoglio, *The War in Abyssinia* (New York, 1937); Guido Leto, *OVRA: Fascismo-antifascismo* (Bologna, 1952); and Alessandro Lessona, *Memorie* (Florence, 1958). General de Bono and Marshal Badoglio were Italian commanders in East Africa, and their military memoirs have laudatory introductions by Mussolini. Leto was chief assistant to the head of the Fascist secret police, and Lessona was an under secretary for the colonies.

Denis Mack Smith, *Italy* (Ann Arbor, Mich., 1959), is a good recent historical survey of modern Italy and gives especially detailed information on the Fascist era. From an Italian but anti-Mussolini viewpoint is Luigi Salvatorelli and Giovanni Mira, "L'impresa etiopica," *Storia d'Italia nel periodo fascista* (Turin, 1956), pp. 776–844. The Italian Minister in Finland and Switzerland during the crisis has written a temperate defense of Mussolini and Fascism, interesting because of its use of unpublished source materials and its multiplicity of pictures: Attilio Tamaro, *Venti anni di storia, 1922–1943* (Rome, 1943), III.

In sharp contrast to the passionately anti-Fascist Salvemini's *Prelude to World War II* are two books by Luigi Villari, *Storia diplomatica del conflitto italo-etiopico* (Bologna, 1943) and *Italian Foreign Policy Under Mussolini* (New York, 1956). The latter is pathological in its defense of Mussolini. On sanctions Villari wrote: "Thus ended one of the most deplorable episodes in politico-diplomatic history, the unsuccessful attempt to starve a civilized nation of 40,000,000 people into surrender." Balanced but dated is Maxwell H. H. Macartney and Paul Cremona, *Italy's Foreign and Colonial Policy, 1914–1937* (London, 1938).

The best biography of Mussolini is Paolo Monelli, *Mussolini: The Intimate Life of a Demagogue* (New York, 1954). Mussolini's apologia, *Il tempo del bastone e della carota: storia di un anno,* is published in English, edited by Max Ascoli, in *The Fall of Mussolini* (New York, 1948). This short and rambling vendetta contains several revealing flashbacks to the early and mid-1930's. Sympathetic to Mussolini and his government is Yvon de Begnac, *Palazzo Venezia: storia di un regime* (Rome, 1950). Edoardo and Duilio Susmel have edited the works of Il Duce, *Opera omnia di Benito Mussolini* (Florence, 1951–60), in 32 volumes; volume 27, *Dall'inaugurazione della provincia di Littoria alla proclamazione dell'impero* (Florence, 1960), covers the Italo-Ethiopian crisis. Based mostly on this collection, Giorgio Pini and Duilio Susmel have written a three-volume biography, *Mussolini: L'uomo e l'opera*, III, *Dalla dittatura all'impero (1925–1938)* (Florence, 1955).

A book that shows how Italian Fascism affected, and was affected by, the Italo-Ethiopian crisis is Dante L. Germino, *The Italian Fascist Party in Power: A Study in Totalitarian Rule* (Minneapolis, 1959). Felice Guarneri, an economics professor and Mussolini's chief financial adviser, has described in detail the Italian economic position and the problem of sanctions in *Battaglie economiche—tra le due grandi guerre* (Milan, 1953).

Great Britain

British diplomatic records for the period have not been published and are not open for research. *Parliamentary Debates* of the House of Commons, Volumes 295–316, Fifth Series (London, 1935–36), are an important source for opinions and policies of government and opposition. British newspapers were more representative of party viewpoints than American and were quite outspoken on the Italo-Ethiopian crisis. I used *The Times* and the *Daily Telegraph* for Conservative and government views, the *News-Chronicle* and the *Manchester Guardian* for Liberal policy, the *Daily Mail* for right-wing Conservative opinion, and the *Daily Herald*, the official organ of the Labour party.

Unlike the Italian and French memoirs, the many British memoirs nearly all discuss the role of the United States in the Italo-Ethiopian crisis. As in the French memoirs, however, the conclusions reached are determined largely by the writer's attitude toward the League of Nations and the proposed oil sanction. In order of usefulness, the more important memoirs are *Nine Troubled Years* (London, 1954), the frank apologia of Samuel Hoare (Viscount Templewood), British Foreign Secretary from June to December 1935; *The Mist Procession: The Autobiography of Lord Vansittart* (London, 1958), by Robert Vansittart, the Permanent Undersecretary of the Foreign Office; *Front-Line Diplomat* (London, 1959), by Geoffrey Thompson, an Ethiopian expert in the Foreign Office; *Both Sides of the Curtain* (London, 1950), by Maurice Peterson, head of the Abyssinian Department of the Foreign Office; *My Political Life*, III, *The Unforgiving Years, 1929–1940* (London, 1955), by Leopold S. Amery, a right-wing Conservative; *A Great Experiment: An Autobiography* (London, 1941), by Robert Cecil, the leading British advocate of the League of Nations; *As It Happened* (London, 1954), by Clement R. Attlee, the Labour leader in Parliament after September 1935; *Retrospect* (London, 1952), by John Simon, Foreign Secretary until June 1935 and then Home Secretary; and Winston S. Churchill, *The Gathering Storm* (Boston, 1948). The second volume of Anthony Eden's memoirs, *Facing the Dictators* (London, 1962), is disappointing.

Two biographies with extensive quotations from letters or diaries are Keith Feiling, *The Life of Neville Chamberlain* (London, 1947), and Charles Petrie, *The Life and Letters of the Right Hon. Sir Austen Chamberlain* (London, 1940), II. Other biographies of interest are Alan Campbell-Johnson, *Eden: The Making of a Statesman* (New York, 1955), and George M. Young, *Stanley Baldwin* (London, 1952).

Charles L. Mowat, *Britain Between the Wars, 1918–1940* (London, 1955), presents an excellent background picture for both domestic politics and international currents. On British-American relations, but with little mention of the Italo-Ethiopian crisis, is Harry C. Allen, *Great Britain and the United States: A History of Anglo-American Relations (1783–1952)* (London, 1954). Specifically on the Labour party are Elaine Windrich, *British Labour's Foreign Policy* (Stanford, Calif., 1952); Henry Pelling, *America and the British Left* (London, 1956); Eugene J. Meehan, *The British Left Wing and Foreign Policy* (New Brunswick, N.J., 1960). A partisan indictment of the ruling Conservative party's handling of foreign affairs is Alfred L. Rowse, *Appeasement: A Study in Political Decline, 1933–1939* (New York, 1961). On British public opinion, see Paul Vaucher and Paul-Henri Siriex, *L'opinion britannique, la Société des Nations, et la guerre italo-éthiopienne* (Paris, 1936).

France

The French diplomatic records, like the British, have not yet been opened or published. Of value for political debates and explanations of policies is *Journal officiel, Débats parlementaires, Chambre des députés* (Paris, 1935–36). The French memoirs, like the Italian, rarely mention the role of the United States in the Italo-Ethiopian crisis. The most useful for France's position are *Politique française: 1919–1940* (Paris, 1947), by Pierre-Etienne Flandin, either Premier or Foreign Minister during most of the crisis; *L'histoire jugera* (Paris, 1945), by Léon Blum, Socialist leader and Premier from June 1936; *Mission à Rome: Mussolini* (Paris, 1955), by Hubert Lagardelle, a French diplomat in Rome, 1933–37; *The Fateful Years* (New York, 1949), by André François-Poncet, French Ambassador to Germany; *In the Thick of the Fight: 1930–1945* (New York, 1955), by Paul Reynaud, a staunch opponent of Laval and advocate of the League of Nations and cooperation with Great Britain; *Entre deux guerres: souvenirs sur la IIIᵉ république, III, Sur les chemins de la défaite, 1935–1940* (Paris, 1946), by Joseph Paul-Boncour, Delegate at Geneva; and *De la Place de la Concorde au cours de l'intendance* (Paris, 1942), by Jean Fabry, Minister of War.

On the controversial role of Pierre Laval, David Thomson, *Two Frenchmen: Pierre Laval and Charles de Gaulle* (London, 1951), does not mince words but is more objective than the pro-Laval Alfred Mallet, *Pierre Laval* (Paris, 1955), I, or the bitterly anti-Laval Henry Torrès, *Pierre Laval* (New York, 1941). Laval's own book, *The Diary of Pierre Laval* (New York, 1948), is only a series of self-justificatory essays written before his trial in 1945.

The internal affairs of France in this period are well covered in several important books. Alexander Werth, *Which Way France?* (London, 1937), is an unusually good contemporary, journalistic account. For French politics Charles A. Micaud, *The French Right and Nazi Germany, 1933–1939* (Durham, N.C., 1943), is excellent. Also useful are François Goguel, *La politique des partis sous la IIIᵉ république* (Paris, 1958), 3d edition, and John T. Marcus, *French Socialism in the Crisis Years, 1933–1936* (New York, 1958). On French public opinion there is a contemporary monograph by Yves Simon, *La campagne d'Ethiopie et la pensée politique française* (Lille, 1936).

The French attitude toward the United States and the American role in the Italo-Ethiopian crisis is demonstrated most clearly in the partisan Paris press. Most valuable are *Le Figaro* and *Le Temps* for conservative views, *Le Populaire* for the Socialist view, and *L'Humanité* for the Communist. *Le Temps* generally spoke for the government, and Léon Blum wrote many of the editorials for *Le Populaire*.

Miscellaneous

The Ethiopian viewpoint was rarely expressed in print. The reports of the American Chargé W. Perry George and Minister Resident Cornelius

Van H. Engert and articles by such journalists as George Steer of the *New York Times* are good places to start, since all three reported sympathetically on the Ethiopian plight. Also available but superficial are *The Abyssinia I Knew* (London, 1936), by General Virgin, a Swedish officer and Haile Selassie's military adviser, and *A Doctor Without a Country* (New York, 1939), by Thomas A. Lambie, an American medical missionary and friend of the Emperor. John M. Melly, "Ethiopia and the War from the Ethiopian Point of View," *International Affairs*, XV (January 1936), 103–21, is a sympathetic defense of Haile Selassie and his country by a British medical missionary. The *Ethiopia Observer* has devoted several issues to Italo-Ethiopian relations: Volume II, Number 11 (October 1957), "The Battle of Adowa," and Volume III, Numbers 10–12, and Volume IV, Number 1 (September–December 1959), "The Italo-Ethiopian War and the Patriotic Struggle." The *Ethiopia Observer* was edited and published in Great Britain and Ethiopia by Sylvia Pankhurst and her son, Richard K. P. Pankhurst. The authors' enthusiasm for things Ethiopian must be kept in mind.

On Ethiopia in general there are two recent surveys: Edward Ullendorff, *The Ethiopians* (London, 1960), and George A. Lipsky, *Ethiopia* (New Haven, Conn., 1962). Ullendorff is a specialist in Ethiopic languages, and Lipsky's work is a part of the Human Relations Area File series. Margery Perham, *The Government of Ethiopia* (New York, 1953), is a study of Ethiopian government and institutions as of 1935, the last year before the Fascist conquest. Ethiopia on the international stage is the subject of a short monograph by Ernest Work, *Ethiopia: A Pawn in European Diplomacy* (New Concord, Ohio, 1935).

The role of the Soviet Union in the Italo-Ethiopian crisis is discussed briefly in T. A. Taracouzio, *War and Peace in Soviet Diplomacy* (New York, 1940); Max Beloff, *The Foreign Policy of Soviet Russia, 1929–1941* (London, 1947), I; and Wladyslaw W. Kulski, *Peaceful Co-Existence: An Analysis of Soviet Foreign Policy* (Chicago, 1959). On Germany, besides the previously cited memoirs of American Ambassador Dodd and French Ambassador François-Poncet, Paul Schmidt, *Hitler's Interpreter* (New York, 1951), and Erich Kordt, *Nicht aus den akten* (Stuttgart, 1950), are useful. The German documents have been published only until the end of March 1935; see *Documents on German Foreign Policy*, Series C (1933–37), "The Third Reich: First Phase," III (Washington, D.C., 1959).